Editor
Mary Kaye Taggart

Editorial Project Manager
Jodi McClay, M.A.

Editorial Manager
Karen Goldfluss, M.S. Ed.

Editor-in-Chief
Sharon Coan, M.S. Ed.

Illustrator
Blanca Apodaca

Cover Artist
Denise Bauer

Art Coordinator
Cheri Macoubrie Wilson

Creative Director
Elayne Roberts

Imaging
James Edward Grace
Stephanie A. Salcido

Product Manager
Phil Garcia

Publishers
Rachelle Cracchiolo, M.S. Ed.
Mary Dupuy Smith, M.S. Ed.

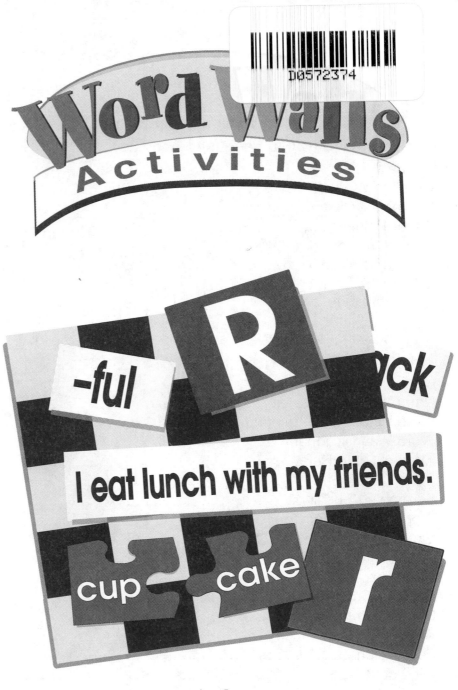

Word Walls Activities

Authors

Dawn Campbell, M.A., and Karen Halderman
Introduction by *Evangelyn Visser*

Teacher Created Materials, Inc.
6421 Industry Way
Westminster, CA 92683
www.teachercreated.com

©2000 Teacher Created Materials, Inc.
Reprinted, 2003

Made in U.SA.
ISBN-1-57690-481-4

Table of Contents

Table of Contents *(cont.)*

Introduction

Importance of Literacy

There was a time when just being able to write your name was considered literate. However, when the printing press was invented, people began to recognize the importance of literacy and began to teach students how to read. Today, with the explosion of information, people must be very good readers to survive economically, and every day these demands increase.

Teachers are under the microscope as parents and politicians demand accountability and student success. All agree that for our country to continue to be successful, its citizens must be literate. Everyone seems to have an opinion about the best way to accomplish literacy for all citizens. Although this debate continues, there is a great deal that is known about what a good reader does and the skills and strategies a child must learn to become a good reader.

It is critical that children receive the most knowledgeable and effective literacy teaching because students who are not independent readers by the end of the third grade are handicapped (Stanovich, 1986). Dependent readers are not motivated to practice something that causes them to struggle. As a result, they do not become good readers.

Reading Is a Complex Process

Learning to read can be a very difficult and overwhelming process. First, students must remember the names and sounds associated with the squiggles and lines of ink line (letters). These squiggles and lines are unique only in relationship to the horizontal line. Some are mirror images of others (*b* and *d*, *q* and *p*). Some are the same except for small details (*n* and *h*, *r* and *n*). Some are flipped over (*w* and *m*, *u* and *n*). Some hint at the sounds that they stand for at the beginnings of their names (*t* and *b*), some at the end (*n*, *f*, and *l*), and some not at all (*h*, *w*, and *y*). Many students are more familiar with uppercase letters, but these often do not look anything like their lowercase partners. This can make reading more difficult because almost all of the letters in most of the text they read are lowercase.

Introduction *(cont.)*

Reading Is a Complex Process *(cont.)*

Besides learning the letters, students must be able to recognize familiar patterns of letters. M. J. Adams calls this the orthographic processor in *Beginning to Read: Thinking and Learning About Print* (1990). The orthographic processor takes individual letters as input and responds to the familiarity of the ordered string by linking the letters together into letter patterns. The strength and speed of the orthographic processor's response to a word depend upon two factors: the speed and adequacy with which the individual letters are perceived and the familiarity of the spelling patterns comprising the word (Adams, 1990).

A third component to learning to read is when the brain uses the letter or multiletter information to retrieve the possible pronunciations of the letter or spelling pattern. How accurately and quickly the student processes the orthographic (letter, letter group) information, the number of possible pronunciations of that letter or letter group, and whether the student is familiar with the appropriate response determines how well this phonological processing works (Adams, 1990).

The last thing a reader needs is the ability to pull all of these components together to create meaning. If a reader is unable to efficiently put the information together, little meaning results. This then defeats the purpose of learning to read in the first place.

Learning to Read

Two basic approaches to teaching reading have developed. The first approach begins with the parts and progresses to the whole. In other words, the approach starts with letter names, then sounds, then blends the sounds together to identify the simple (consonant, vowel, consonant) words, then adds more complex patterns. This is generally recognized as the *phonics* method.

The second approach is called the *whole word* method. In this method, the student works on a given set of words until the words are recalled automatically. Reading material is designed with as much repetition of these words as possible without losing all meaning. Flash cards and repeated readings take advantage of the brain's ability to recall conditioned responses. This is sometimes called the hot stove effect (Jensen, 1998).

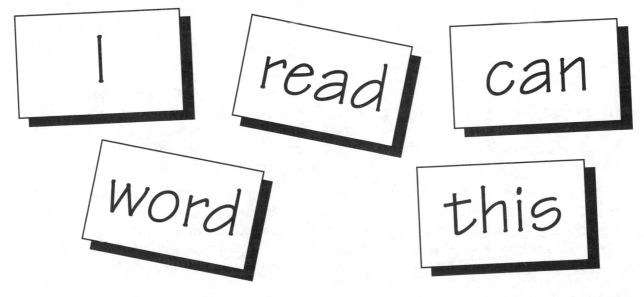

Introduction *(cont.)*

Good readers who learn to read with just the whole word method must infer the correspondence between different patterns and what the words and word parts sound like orally. Some students do not make this connection without instruction. They are faced with learning each word as a unique symbol or logogram, similar to Chinese logograms. Obviously, learning all 600,000 English words this way is overwhelming, if not impossible. Even learning the 5,000 words that make up 90% of a school child's running text would be difficult. The reader that could accomplish this task would be absolutely confounded by the other 10% of the words which carry most of the meaning. And because of the large number of words in this group, the chances of encountering the word often enough to learn it would not occur (Carrol, Davies, and Richman, 1971).

Good readers who learn to read with phonics, must develop a large number of instantly recognizable words, both phonetic and nonphonetic. They must also transition from sounding out letter by letter sequentially to chunking (using the words or word parts they know) to attack multisyllabic words. This recognition of familiar patterns and relationships among different words is also called *structural analysis.* This is a critical component of making the jump between either the whole word method or pure phonics to good reading. Unfortunately, in the past, teaching this critical skill was left until third grade or later (Bishop and Bishop, 1996). Some advocate that this analysis take place alongside beginning reading instruction.

Onset and Rimes

Children are able to recognize syllables. Students can learn, perhaps as the result of learning to read, to separate syllables into separate sounds. How do children get from syllables to total segmentation? When researchers asked subjects to separate syllables, they consistently separated a syllable between the beginning consonant or consonant cluster and the remaining letters in the syllable.

Further study revealed that there is a limited number of possible beginning and ending consonants or consonant clusters; for example, syllables can begin with *gr* but not end with it or end with *ng* but not begin with it. In learning language, there are many words that begin with *st*, such as *stay, stop, stair, stomp,* and *still,* and many that end with *ing*, such as *thing, sing, ring, bring,* and *string.* But there is only one word that begins with *st* and ends with *ing,* and that word is *sting.* So in terms of patterns, the brain has received many more repetitions of *st* hanging together and *ing* hanging together than it has of the entire word *sting* hanging together.

This separation is called *onset* (the beginning consonants) and *rime* (the remaining pattern of letters). This has significance in learning words. The limited number of beginning and ending consonant(s) is a discrete set that can be learned. In addition, R. E. Wylie and D. D. Durrell point out in *Elementary English* (1970) that nearly 500 primary grade words can be derived from a set of only 37 rimes. These rimes are listed on page 176.

By focusing on these two discrete sets and presenting activities that give the students more exposure to these patterns, the teacher helps the students move from recognizing single letters to recognizing letter clusters. This also helps when multisyllabic words are encountered. The reader knows to break words where unlikely letter combinations appear (for example, *rl* is such a combination, and the word *nearly* is parsed into *near-ly*).

Introduction *(cont.)*

Compound Words

Compound words are words that are made up of two smaller words. They are a good way to introduce students to multisyllabic words. Again, this is a way to train the mind and the eye to look for familiar words or rimes within longer words.

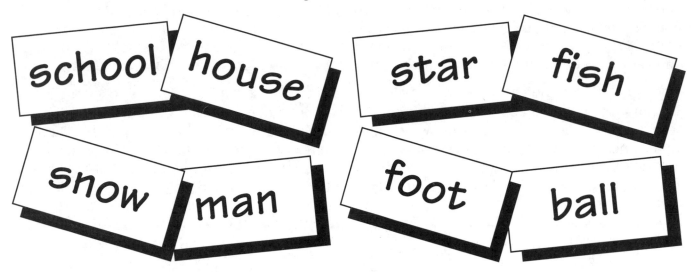

Affixes (Prefixes and Suffixes)

Affixes are letter groups that are added to the beginnings or endings of words. They include verb endings and plural endings. Some prefixes and suffixes change the meanings of words or change their uses (for example, from noun to verb). The activities presented help the students group letters and also help them develop strategies to deal with the meanings of unknown words.

Pronunciation

Coming up with a probable pronunciation for a word such as Penelope (Pen-e-lope) is using structural analysis. There is the three-letter word *Pen*, and the last four letters look like *hope*, and the *e* is an unstressed syllable that likely would be pronounced as a *schwa* (ə). Some students make these types of connections without instruction, but some students need explicit instruction. Showing students how to use words that they know how to pronounce to get to possible pronunciations of new words is very helpful. Students have learned the meanings of thousands of words by hearing them used in various ways. It follows that this same process occurs for developing definitions for new words that are read.

Word Walls

Because good readers need to use letter recognition skills, high-frequency words, and structural analysis, a balanced program must include ways to strengthen these skills for all students. The activities in this book provide students with a myriad of ways to work with words. Putting words on the wall is not a new idea. There are wall dictionaries, thematic word lists, word family lists, doozers (McCracken and McCracken, 1995), color charts, number charts, and labeling. However, P. M. Cunningham in *Phonics They Use* (1995) advocates setting up a permanent bulletin board and developing activities using these words as an important part of word work.

Introduction *(cont.)*

Who's Counting?

Studies have shown that 50% of the words a student reads are made up of just 109 words (Carrol, Davies, and Richman, 1971). So, when students learn these words and can recall them automatically, 50% of the word processing part of reading has been accomplished. In addition, these words provide anchors. These anchors give students time to consider meaning instead of struggling to recognize the next word.

Variety

One way to learn these 109 words is with flash cards. This is classic stimulus-response learning. However, teachers know that this method does not work with every student. It completely disregards what we know about multimodal learning, multiple intelligences, and the importance of play. *Word Wall Activities* gives teachers the means to teach these words to students in a variety of ways. By participating in these activities every day, students learn the words in a nonthreatening, playful way.

Other Benefits

Many children learn their letters when an adult writes down what the child dictates. This is especially true if the adult spells the word aloud as it is written. This can be replicated with the word wall by spelling the word and pointing to the letters.

Spelling words with rhythm or associating the letters with physical signals (cheerleading style) helps children who find it easier to recall information if it is stored in the body (kinesthetic) or learned musically.

Handwriting can be taught and practiced using the word wall. This is particularly valuable because it gives children the opportunity to analyze how the letters look in comparison to each other—tall, short, round, dropping below the line, etc.

Structural analysis can be addressed by choosing a useful word from the word wall (or adding a new word to the word wall along with high-frequency words) and having the students create new words from parts of this known word. For example, the students might find and write the word *car* from the word wall. Then the students could list *far*, *jar*, *tar*, *star*, and *stars*. Some students figure out how to do this easily. For others, it takes weeks and months of repetition to see how word parts from known words can help them spell and read unfamiliar words.

Games

Many of the activities in this book are in the form of games. This is because games increase learning. Passive games can increase gains by 30%, active games by as much as 53% (May, 1990). This makes sense. When students are involved in games, they are on task, they have peer support (intellectually and socially), and they receive instant feedback. In addition, the fun makes the task much less stressful, which encourages the brain to remember (Jacobs and Nadel, 1985).

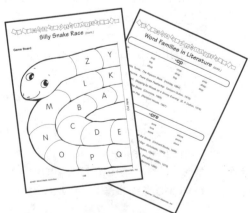

Introduction *(cont.)*

How to Use This Book

The remaining portion of this book includes activities that address use of the word wall, learning high-frequency words, and structural analysis. The activities are designed to supplement an existing reading program. For some of the activities, there are helpful word lists which can be used in conjunction with the activities.

Notice the letter(s) at the bottom of each page. These denote whether the lesson is geared toward an individual student (I), a pair of students (P), a small group (S), or a whole class (W). Many activities could work with several configurations (e.g., whole group, small group, or individual), and this will also be indicated at the bottom of each page.

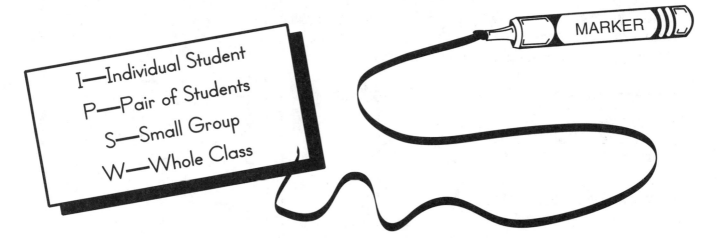

I—Individual Student
P—Pair of Students
S—Small Group
W—Whole Class

MARKER

Beginning on page 16, you will find activities that will help your students practice their word skills. Many of these activities can be introduced by using the word wall. Students not only need to practice high-frequency words, but they also need to practice word concepts to help them increase their reading fluency. The word concepts that are included in this book are listed below. The column of page numbers (below) tells where you can find the beginnings of these sections. Lists of words that are examples of these concepts can be found on the first pages of each section. The lists will also be useful to you if you should choose to create word walls which focus on these concepts.

Steps for Making a Word Wall an Integral Part of Your Classroom

Word walls can be small or large, formal or informal, depending on your style and the area available to you. They can be created by you or store bought. No matter what type of space is available to you, a word wall can be a valuable asset to your classroom.

Step 1: Finding a Location

Look around your room. Find an area that is accessible and easily visible to all students in the room. It can be a . . .

- bulletin board

- chalkboard

- side of a filing cabinet

- closet door

- back of a bookshelf

- chart stand

- roll-away felt board

Step 2: Choosing Your Words

Words can be found in a variety of places. You can use high-frequency words such as the ones on page 23 or pages 204–207. You can also use difficult and hard-to-spell words as well as words that do not have any intrinsic meanings by themselves (*the, as*). You can use words that reflect a classroom theme, a curricular area, or a story. You could also use spelling words, words from a word family (*at, pat, cat*), words that teach a particular language concept (homophones, synonyms, etc.), or words used frequently from your students' writings and interests.

Choose up to 10 words to work with weekly. You may want to start more slowly; it will depend on your class.

Steps for Making a Word Wall an Integral Part of Your Classroom *(cont.)*

Step 3: Preparing Your Words

Now that you have chosen your words, there are a variety of ways to prepare them for display. You may wish to use colored index cards for each week. You may also use die-cut blocks to cut out individual letters. Transferred letters and computer generated words also work well. You may wish to highlight certain patterns in the words, such as silent letters or word family patterns, or you might want to cut out each word around its ascenders and descenders. This helps the students to visually distinguish among possibly confusing words. No matter what method you use, make sure the words are clearly written. The choice is up to you!

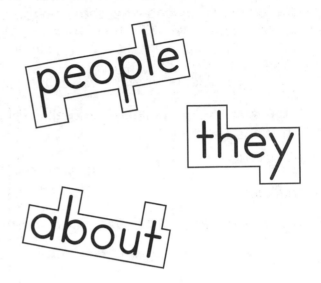

Step 4: Introducing Your Words

Day 1

Hold up the words one by one. Read the words. Count the number of letters. Look at the ascenders and descenders. As Patricia Cunningham suggests in *Classrooms that Work* (1995), chant and clap the words orally as a class. Students might enjoy creating their own rhythms for each word. A variation on this is to have students take a step for each letter and jump when they say the final word.

Days 2–5

There are many ways to quickly practice the words each day. Below are some possible activities (both oral and written) to choose from.

1. Have the students discover the new words on the word wall.

2. After you have introduced the words, extra copies can be printed and given to the students. To excuse students to recess, centers, etc., call out a word and ask the students to look through their word collections to locate the word. Then dismiss them as they reveal the correct word.

3. Practice writing the words in the air.

4. Call on students to use the word wall words in sentences (orally or written).

5. Provide clues to a word, and ask the students to try to guess it. **Example:** This word begins with a *c* and rhymes with *hat*.

Steps for Making a Word Wall an Integral Part of Your Classroom (cont.)

6. Call out a synonym, antonym, or rhyme of one of the word wall words. Have the students try to guess what the word is.

7. Clap, chant, and write the words (Cunningham, 1995).

8. Have the students write the words in alphabetical order.

9. Challenge the students to guess a missing word by considering the context of an unfinished sentence.

   Example: Write an *s* on the board. Say, "The first word begins with *s* and fits in this sentence—I _____ an airplane flying by." (Cunningham, 1995)

10. Make flash cards of the words and sort them in the following ways (Gruber, 1998):

> beginning and ending sounds
>
> beginning and ending blends
>
> ending rimes
>
> alphabetical order
>
> vowel sounds and combinations
>
> singular and plural
>
> number of syllables
>
> number of letters

Steps for Making a Word Wall an Integral Part of Your Classroom *(cont.)*

11. Give the students several minutes to study the words on the word wall. Then ask them to close their eyes while you cover up parts of the words with small, sticky papers. Call on volunteers to identify the missing letters of the words. After the letters are correctly identified, remove the sticky papers and have the class spell the words together (Gruber, 1998).

12. Think of five clues to go with one of the word wall words. Have the students number their papers 1–5. Start reading your clues aloud. The clues should become progressively more specific so that by the fifth clue there can only be one answer. With each clue the students must write down a guess. Once the students feel they have the right answer, they should keep writing the same answer until all of the clues have been given.

Sample Clue Set

1. It is one of the words on the word wall.

2. It has three letters.

3. It begins with an s.

4. The vowel in it is a.

5. It finishes the sentence, "I _____ on the chair."

Using Your Word Wall in Language Activities

Most of this book is devoted to suggesting longer activities for practicing word wall words. These activities can be used in small or whole group situations. Use and adapt whichever activities work best for you and your students. Remember that teaching sight words is an important task as long as the students understand the meanings and/or uses of the words they are learning (Bishop, 1996).

Reading Books with High-Frequency Words

Shared reading is a good time to reinforce high-frequency words. Eeds (1985) provides a list of books which contain a high percentage of her "bookwords." A portion of this list is provided below and on the next page. It lists some books that have the fewest number of different words. For example, *Snake In, Snake Out* has 38 running words, but there is a total of only eight different words in the book. As the students read these books, they will encounter and practice high-utility words on a regular basis (Bishop and Bishop, 1996).

Author	Title	Total Words	Different Words
Alexander, Martha	*Blackboard Bear* (Dial, 1988,)	128	62
Alexander, Martha	*Move Over, Twerp* (Dial, 1989)	245	107
Allard, Harry and James Marshall	*The Stupids Die* (Houghton Mifflin, 1985)	296	140
Allard, Harry	*The Stupids Step Out* (Houghton Mifflin, 1977)	413	176
Asch, Frank	*Sand Cake* (Gareth Stevens, 1993)	443	153
Banchek, Linda	*Snake In, Snake Out* (Dell, 1992)	38	8
Barton, Byron	*Where's Al?* (Houghton Mifflin, 1989)	34	18
Bornstein, Ruth	*Little Gorilla* (Houghton Mifflin, 1986)	173	80
Brandenburg, Fritz	*I Wish I Was Sick Too* (Morrow, 1990)	327	107
Breinburg, Petronella	*Shawn Goes to School* (HarperCollins, 1974)	132	75
Brown, Margaret Wise	*The Runaway Bunny* (HarperCollins Children's, 1991)	441	83
Buckley, Helen	*Grandfather and I* (Lothrop, 1994)	291	79
Burningham, John	*Avocado Baby* (HarperCollins, 1994)	373	160
Burningham, John	*Mr. Grumpy's Outing* (Holt, 1995)	289	95
Burningham, John	*The Blanket* (Candlewick, 1994)	66	33

Using Your Word Wall in Language Activities *(cont.)*

Author	Title	Total Words	Different Words
Burningham, John	*The Dog* (Candlewick, 1994)	69	48
Burningham, John	*The Friend* (Candlewick, 1994)	51	34
Clifton, Lucille	*Everett Anderson's Goodbye* (Holt, 1995)	200	104
Cohen, Miriam	*Will I Have a Friend?* (Simon & Schuster Children's, 1989)	464	277
Delton, Judy	*New Girl at School* (Dutton, 1979)	379	158
dePaola, Tomie	*The Knight and the Dragon* (Putnam, 1992)	129	65
Flack, Marjorie	*Ask Mr. Bear* (Aladdin, 1986)	632	118
Ginsberg, Mirra	*The Chick and the Duckling* (Simon & Schuster Children's, 1988)	112	30
Griffith, Helen	*Mine Will, Said John* (Greenwillow, 1992)	506	124
Hoban, Russell and Lillian	*The Stone Doll of Sister Brute* (Dell, 1992)	494	143
Hutchins, Pat	*The Surprise Party* (Simon & Schuster Children's, 1991)	336	101
Keats, Ezra Jack	*Goggles!* (Viking Penguin, 1998)	336	139
Keats, Ezra Jack	*Whistle for Willie* (Puffin, 1977)	391	149
Kellogg, Steven	*Pinkerton Behave* (Dial, 1993)	233	116
Kraus, Robert	*Leo the Late Bloomer* (HarperCollins Children's, 1998)	166	70
Kraus, Robert	*Whose Mouse Are You?* (Simon & Schuster Children's, 1986)	108	54
Lionni, Leo	*Little Blue and Little Yellow* (Morrow, 1995)	284	123
Marshall, James	*George and Martha* (Houghton Mifflin, 1974)	645	210
Mayer, Mercer	*There's a Nightmare in My Closet* (Puffin, 1992)	142	76
Sendak, Maurice	*Where the Wild Things Are* (HarperCollins, 1992)	350	129
Udry, Janice	*Let's Be Enemies* (Turtleback, 1998)	229	102
Wells, Rosemary	*Noisy Nora* (Dial), 1997	206	101

Ride the Word Waves

Purpose

Word waves are lists of high-frequency words formed in a wave shape. The students will enjoy practicing their words as they ride the waves.

Materials

- copies of pages 17–22 (Choose one, some, or all of these pages according to your needs.)

- highlighters

Preparation

You may want to make two copies per child of each of the word waves lists. This will allow them to have one copy at home and one at school. Instructions for the parents are on each page. If you do not want to include these on the classroom copies, cover them up before you make the photocopies.

Instructions

The student should start on the left side of the page and read as many words as he or she can, ascending and then descending the waves. The student should be able to recognize and identify the words on sight. When a student comes to a word that gives him or her difficulty, he or she stops there. Highlight the last word correctly read and date it. (See page 23 for a word list variation.)

Cleanup

Store copies of each student's Ride the Word Waves pages in a three-ring binder. Send one copy home if you wish.

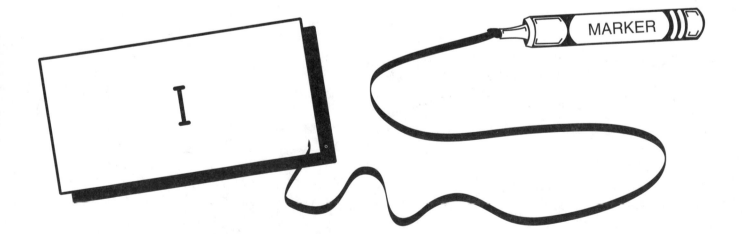

Ride the Word Waves *(cont.)*

they
his
with
as
are
on
for
was

I
at
be
this
have
from
or
one
had
he
it
that
you
is
in
to
a
and
of
the

when
we
were
all
what
not
but
word
by

your

can
there
use
an
each
which
she

said
their
if
how
do

Dear Parent,

This is a list of sight words that your child should learn to read. Each evening, ask your child to begin reading from the waves at the left side of the page. When your child reaches a word that gives him or her difficulty, stop there. Circle (or highlight) and date the last correctly read word.

Ride the Word Waves (cont.)

Dear Parent,

This is a list of sight words that your child should learn to read. Each evening, ask your child to begin reading from the waves at the left side of the page. When your child reaches a word that gives him or her difficulty, stop there. Circle (or highlight) and date the last correctly read word.

Ride the Word Waves *(cont.)*

give
most
very after thing
our
just
good name
sentence
man
think
say
great
where before
help much
through
mean old
too
right
line
any
same
tell
follow
came boy small
want show set
around
also
three
form

back
me
live
year
place
know
work
little
only
take
sound
new

Dear Parent,

This is a list of sight words that your child should learn to read. Each evening, ask your child to begin reading from the waves at the left side of the page. When your child reaches a word that gives him or her difficulty, stop there. Circle (or highlight) and date the last correctly read word.

Ride the Word Waves *(cont.)*

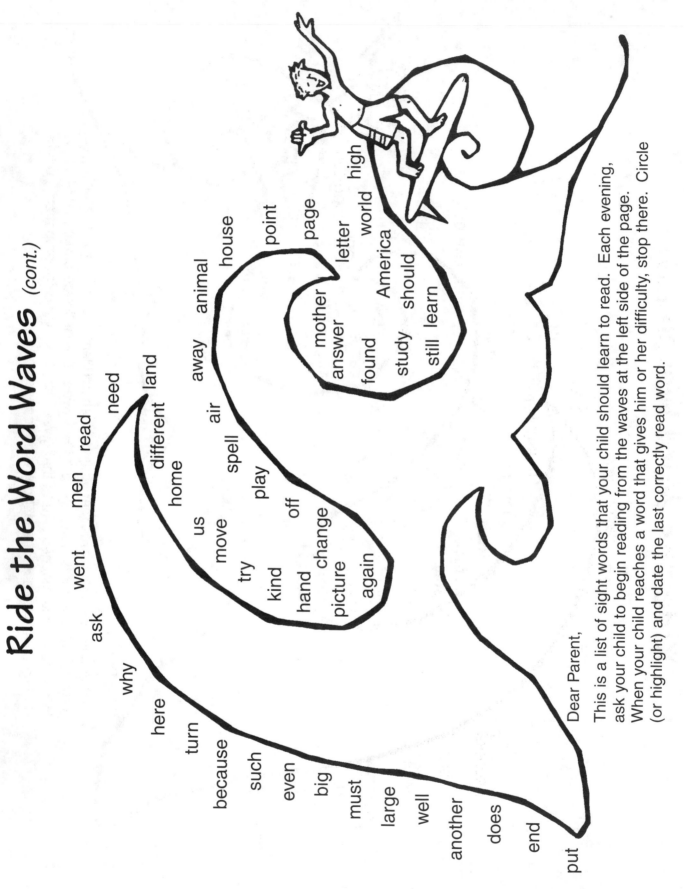

high

page
letter
world
America
mother   should
answer   study
found   still   learn

house
point
animal
away

land
need
read
men
went   different
ask   home
         air
         us
         move   spell
         try   play
why   kind   off
here   hand   change
turn   picture
because   again
such
even
big
must
large
well
another
does
end
put

Dear Parent,

This is a list of sight words that your child should learn to read. Each evening, ask your child to begin reading from the waves at the left side of the page. When your child reaches a word that gives him or her difficulty, stop there. Circle (or highlight) and date the last correctly read word.

Ride the Word Waves (cont.)

tree never start city earth eye thought light keep father school last plant country below own between food add near every

head under story saw something left don't few while close might along

next seem hard open example begin those both always important paper run together often got group life

Dear Parent,

This is a list of sight words that your child should learn to read. Each evening, ask your child to begin reading from the waves at the left side of the page. When your child reaches a word that gives him or her difficulty, stop there. Circle (or highlight) and date the last correctly read word.

Ride the Word Waves *(cont.)*

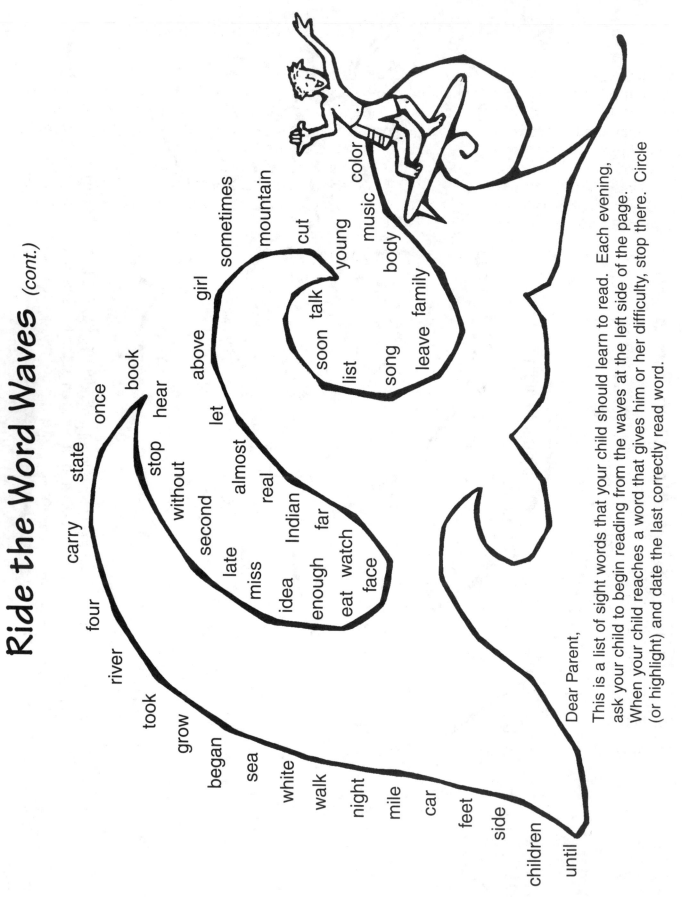

carry state once book
four hear
river stop
took without
grow second let above girl
began late almost sometimes
sea miss real mountain
white idea Indian cut
walk enough far young
night eat watch music color
mile face song body
car list soon talk
feet leave family
side
children
until

Dear Parent,

This is a list of sight words that your child should learn to read. Each evening, ask your child to begin reading from the waves at the left side of the page. When your child reaches a word that gives him or her difficulty, stop there. Circle (or highlight) and date the last correctly read word.

Ride the Word Waves (cont.)

You may choose to create your own set of words to use with Ride the Word Waves. The following list is a compilation of high-frequency words. It was developed by comparing the lists of Carrol, Davies, and Richman (1971), Fry (1980), and Eeds (1985). The 100 words are those that can be located on at least two of the three lists. They are presented in approximate order of use. To be selected for the 50 words of highest frequency, the word must have appeared on all three lists. If students can learn the first 10 words, they will know approximately 25 percent of the words they will encounter when reading. If the students learn all 100 words, they will know approximately 50 percent of the words they will encounter when reading (Bishop and Bishop, 1996).

High-Frequency Words

1. the	21. at	41. do	61. go	81. more
2. and	22. one	42. from	62. about	82. two
3. a	23. said	43. were	63. could	83. day
4. to	24. all	44. so	64. time	84. will
5. in	25. have	45. her	65. look	85. come
6. you	26. what	46. by	66. them	86. get
7. of	27. we	47. if	67. many	87. down
8. it	28. can	48. their	68. see	88. now
9. is	29. this	49. some	69. like	89. little
10. he	30. not	50. then	70. these	90. than
11. that	31. she	51. him	71. me	91. too
12. was	32. your	52. our	72. words	92. first
13. for	33. when	53. an	73. into	93. been
14. I	34. had	54. or	74. use	94. who
15. his	35. as	55. no	75. has	95. people
16. they	36. will	56. my	76. way	96. its
17. with	37. on	57. which	77. bike	97. water
18. are	38. up	58. would	78. make	98. long
19. be	39. out	59. each	79. did	99. find
20. but	40. there	60. how	80. could	100. part

Rainbow Activities

Purpose

Students will practice spelling the word wall words with different colors.

Materials

- paper
- crayons, colored pencils, markers, and/or paints and paintbrushes

Preparation

Prepare a sample and assemble the materials.

Instructions

Rainbow Writing

Ask the students to rainbow-write their weekly words by making each letter of a word a different color. You may have them do this one or more times for each word. As a variation, you may wish to have them color the vowels one color and the consonants another color.

Rainbow Painting

This activity is the same as rainbow writing except the students use paints and brushes or finger paints instead. Display the painted words on the word wall for the week.

Rainbow Shapes

Have the students draw around the shape of each word, following the ascending and descending letters. The students should then repeat this procedure several times, using a different color each time.

Cleanup

Display the completed rainbow activities. Store the pencils, crayons, paints, and paintbrushes in their appropriate containers.

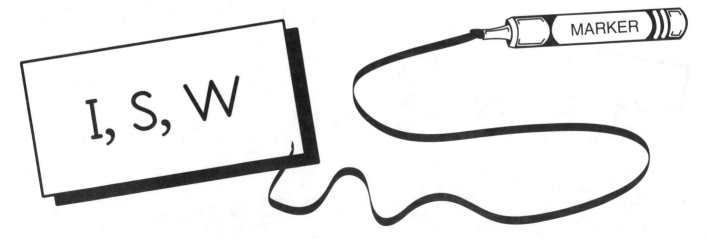

Water Painting

Purpose

Students will use water to practice spelling the word wall words.

Materials

- list of word wall words

- plastic cups

- water

- 1" (2.54 cm)-wide paintbrushes

Preparation

Fill the plastic cups halfway with water. Schedule a time when students can use the playground and not be interrupted.

Instructions

Hand out a paintbrush and a cup of water to each student. Take the students out to the playground or blacktop area. Instruct them to paint (with water only) their word wall words on the blacktop or pavement. Have a list of the words available for their reference.

Cleanup

Discuss the words that the students painted. Rinse out the paintbrushes and dispose of the cups.

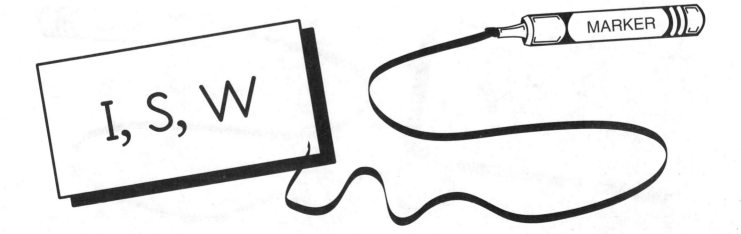

Bounce a Word

Purpose

Students will use a ball to practice spelling their word wall words.

Materials

- rubber balls

Preparation

No preparation is necessary.

Instructions

Give each student a ball and take your class out to the playground. Call out a word wall word to the students. Have the students bounce out each letter as they spell the word out loud in unison.

Cleanup

Collect the balls.

Variations

If you do not have enough rubber balls for all of the students you can . . .

- supplement your supply with tennis balls.

- pair the students and have them bounce one ball back and forth to each other.

- arrange the students in a circle and have them pass and bounce the ball from person to person around the circle.

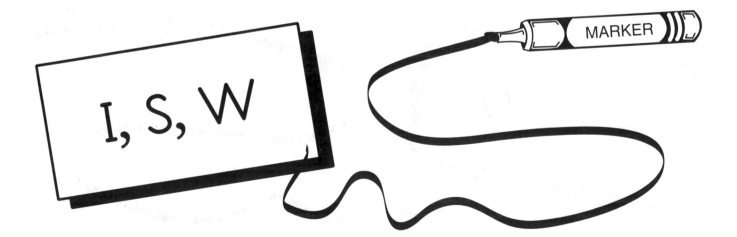

Write and Trace

Purpose

Students will practice tracing their word wall words with wipe-off markers.

Materials

- construction paper

- wipe-off markers

- laminating materials

- bag or box for storage

Preparation

Write each word wall word in large letters on a piece of construction paper. Laminate the words.

Instructions

Pass out the laminated words. Have the students practice tracing their word wall words with wipe-off markers.

Cleanup

Wipe off the laminated words. Store them with the wipe-off markers in a bag or box.

Variations

Challenge the students to write their words in sand, rice, shaving cream, or another interesting medium.

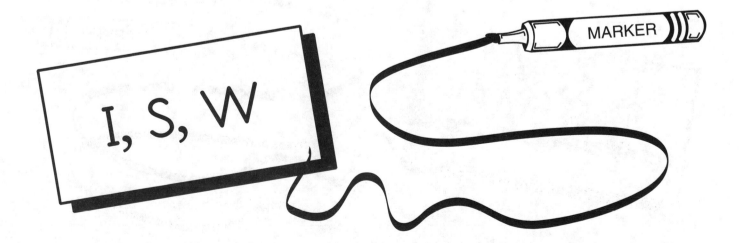

3-D Words

Purpose

Students will use three-dimensional materials to practice spelling their word wall words.

Materials

- alphabet cereal
- alphabet stamps
- magnetic letters
- play dough (See the recipe on page 29.)
- dry macaroni
- dry beans
- large alphabet letters

Preparation

Have all of the above materials collected in a central location. Photocopy the large block letters for the students to spell out word wall words on the floor.

Instructions

Ask the students to practice spelling word wall words by using the above materials. Continue as time permits.

Cleanup

Store the materials in their appropriate areas.

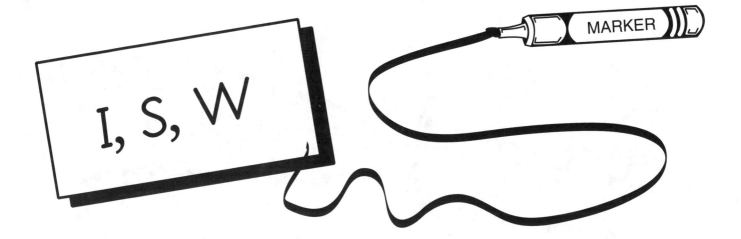

3-D Words *(cont.)*

Homemade Play Dough Recipe

- 1 cup (240 mL) flour

- 1 cup (240 mL) water

- ½ cup (120 mL) salt

- 1 tablespoon (15 mL) cream of tartar

- 1 tablespoon (15 mL) cooking oil

- a few drops of food coloring

Mix all of the ingredients together in a pan and cook on high, stirring constantly. Remove the mixture from the heat when the play dough reaches the correct consistency. Let cool.

Instructions for Play Dough Use

The children can roll the play dough flat with a rolling pin and then cut out various letters, using cookie cutters or dull, plastic knives. They could also mold the dough to create letters and words.

To store the play dough for future use, gather it into a ball (a separate ball for each color) and tightly seal it in a container. Place the cookie cutters and other tools in a basket or bag and store them by the dough.

ACTIVITIES

Mother, May I?

Purpose

Students will use movement to practice spelling their word wall words.

Materials

- a list of word wall words

Preparation

No preparation is necessary.

Instructions

Line up the students at the back of a large, open area. Choose a student to be the leader. The leader stands in front of the group and calls on one of the students. The leader asks him or her to spell a certain word from the word wall. (The leader can use a photocopied list of the words.) If he or she spells the word correctly, the leader will give that person further instructions, such as, "Take three baby steps" or "Take two giant steps." Then the leader will go on to a new student and repeat the process with a new word. If a student misses a word, then the leader goes on to the next student. The game will continue until one person reaches the leader. That student then becomes the new leader.

Cleanup

No cleanup is necessary.

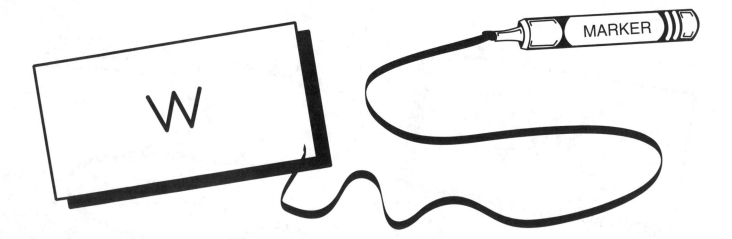

Bingo

Purpose

Students will play a game to practice identifying their word wall words.

Materials

- copies of the bingo cards (page 32 or 33)
- index cards
- pencils
- bingo markers (e.g., poker chips, pennies, squares of paper)

Preparation

Choose one of the two bingo card styles on pages 32 and 33. Photocopy enough cards so that each student has one. Choose which words from the word wall you would like to use for this activity, and write them on the board. Write each of the same words on index cards.

Instructions

Pass out the blank bingo cards to the students. Have the students copy the word wall words onto the squares of their game cards. One at a time, pull and read aloud index cards from the pile. Tell the students to put markers on the words as you call them out. Continue until someone gets an entire row, column, or diagonal covered and calls out "Bingo!"

Cleanup

Collect the game markers and bingo cards and store them in a large manila envelope.

Variations

You could also purchase a sight-word bingo game at your local teacher-supply store.

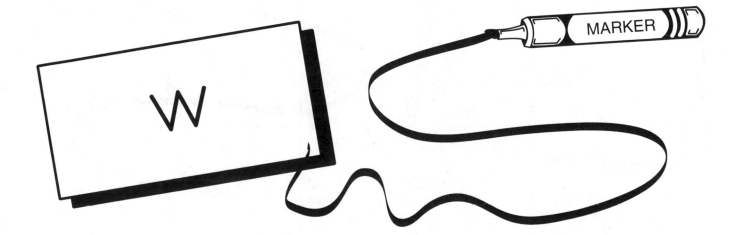

Bingo *(cont.)*

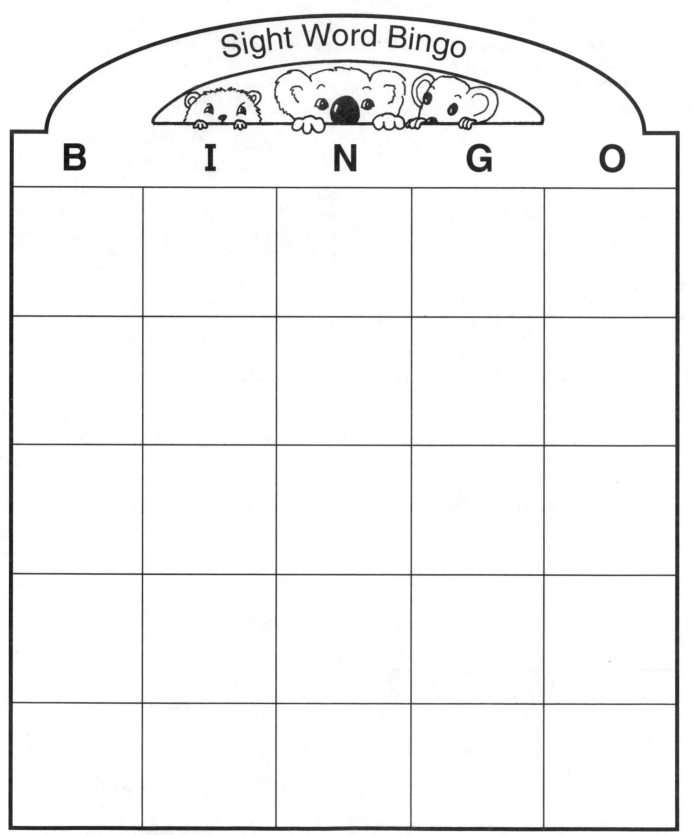

Sight Word Bingo

B	I	N	G	O

Bingo (cont.)

BINGO

Concentration

Purpose

Students will identify and read words from the word wall.

Materials

- colored index cards

- markers

Preparation

Decide which words from the word wall you will use for this activity. Write each word on two index cards. Be sure to use colored index cards and a marker that does not leak through so students will not be able to read the cards when they are flipped over. One set of cards will serve three to four players. Make as many sets as you need for your class.

Instructions

To play this game, the students need to lay the cards out facedown. They then take turns looking for matching pairs of cards. They should try to read the words aloud as they turn them over. If a student finds a matching pair, he or she gets to continue playing. The student continues playing until he or she does not make a match.

After all of the pairs have been uncovered and claimed, the student with the most pairs is declared the winner.

Cleanup

Collect the index cards and store each set in a separate envelope.

Word Walking

Purpose

Students will identify and read words from the word wall.

Materials

- copies of the footprints on page 36

- markers

- laminating materials

- music (optional)

Preparation

Reproduce the footprints on page 36. Write a word from the word wall on each foot. Cut out the prints and laminate them.

Instructions

Lay out the footprints on the ground in a circular walking pattern. Students will walk on the words until someone says "Stop!" Then call on several students (one at a time) to read the words they are standing on and to use them in sentences. Repeat this until every student has had a turn to read one word.

Cleanup

Collect the feet and store them in a resealable, plastic bag.

Variation

Play music while the students are walking on the footprints. Instruct them to freeze when you stop the music. Proceed with the rest of the activity as described above.

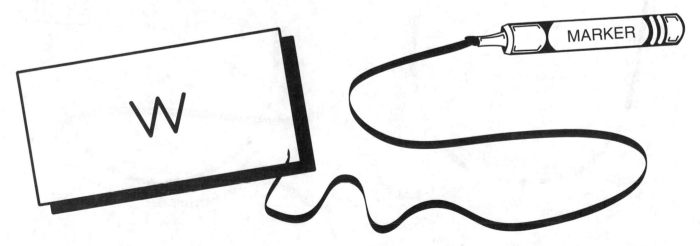

Word Walking (cont.)

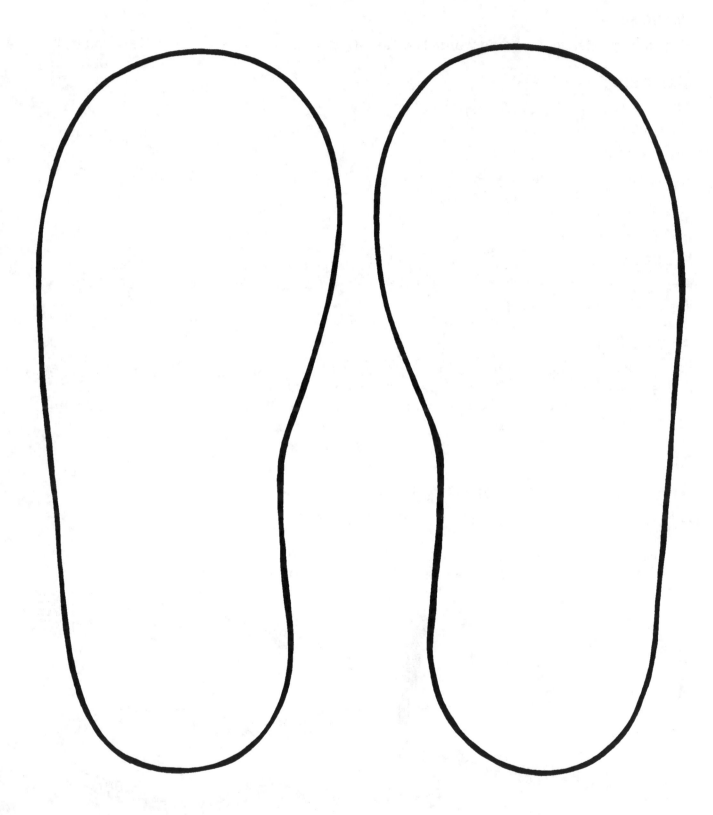

Go Fish for High-Frequency Words

Purpose

The students will play a game to practice identifying and reading words from the word wall.

Materials

- index cards
- markers

Preparation

You will need to write down 13 words from the word wall on index cards, four times each. Be sure to use a marker that cannot be seen through the card.

Instructions

Divide the students into small groups and give each group a deck of prepared word cards. This game is played much as you would the traditional "Go Fish" game. Shuffle the cards. Deal out seven cards to each student; the extras go into the "pond" in the middle of the group, facedown. The first player asks another player for one of the words in his or her hand. "Do you have the word *said*?" The second player looks through his or her cards and either gives the first player the card if he or she has it, or, if not, says, "Go fish." If the card is given to the first player, he or she may ask for additional word cards from any player. When the first player is finally told to "Go fish," the player then draws a card from the "pond." He or she gets one draw. If the word *said* is drawn, the player's turn continues. If the word *said* is not drawn, the player's turn is over, and play continues to the next person. The game continues until a player has matched all of the cards in his or her hand. Whoever has the most matches wins.

Cleanup

Collect the cards, wrap a rubber band around each deck, and store them in an envelope.

Name the Word

Purpose

Students will practice reading and recognizing the words from the word wall.

Materials

- the word wall

Preparation

Invite a small group of students to sit by the word wall.

Instructions

Choose one student to be the *pointer*. The pointer will point to various word wall words and have the other students say the words aloud. This can be done individually or as a group. After a certain number of words, a new pointer will take a turn. Make sure each child has a turn being the pointer.

Cleanup

No cleanup is necessary.

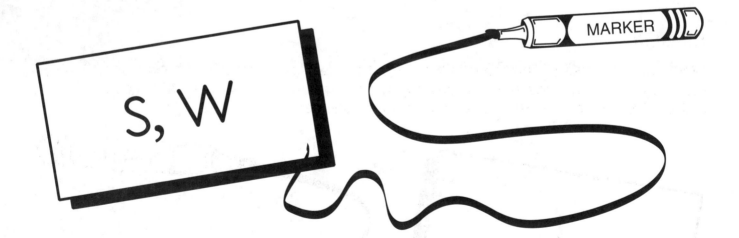

Word Wheel

Purpose

Students will practice reading and recognizing the words from the word wall.

Materials

- flash cards (page 41)
- a copy of the spinner (page 40)
- brad
- scissors
- glue
- markers
- tagboard

Preparation

Make a spinner by copying page 40, cutting out the spinner, and gluing it onto tagboard. Attach the pointer to the center of the spinner with a brad. Write eight words from the word wall on the spinner. Write the same eight words on flash cards (page 41). Reproduce enough flash cards so that the students will each have a copy.

Instructions

Put the flash cards in a pile in the center of the students. The first player spins the spinner. When it stops, the player will read the word. If the player reads the word correctly, he or she receives a flash card with the word on it. The winner will be the first child to collect all of the words.

Cleanup

When the students are finished with the game, they can take their sets of flash cards, staple them together, and study them individually or with partners. Or, the flash cards could be collected for future use. Store the spinner in a plastic bag.

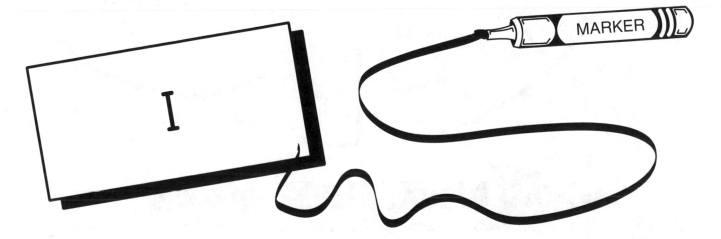

Word Wheel *(cont.)*

Spinner

To make your spinner, reproduce the patterns below and cut them out. Mount them on tagboard and trim the excess board around the edges. Make a hole in the center of the arrow. Place the arrow over the spinner so that the hole is directly over the center dot in the circle. Push the point of the brad's through the dot in the center of the circle. Spread the brad's ends apart. Test your spinner. If the arrow is too tight, adjust the bending points of the brad and/or enlarge the center hole on the arrow.

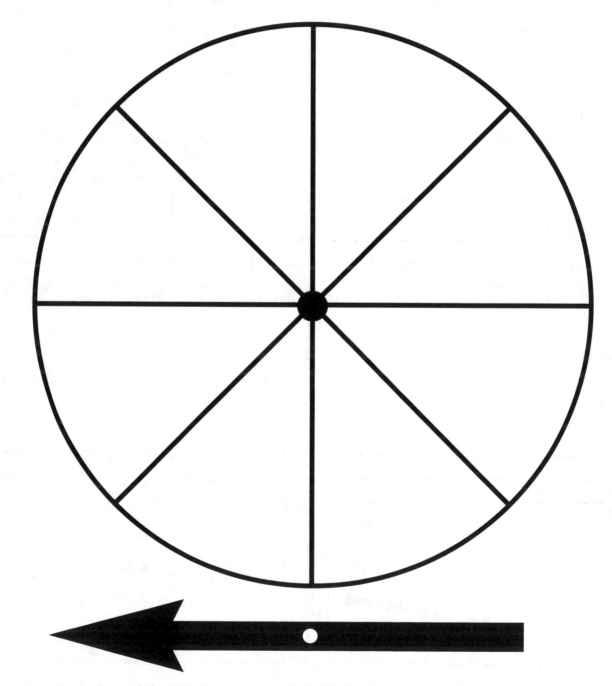

Word Wheel *(cont.)*

Word Wall Dictionary

Purpose

Students will be writing the words from the word wall in a dictionary format.

Materials

- copies of pages 43–69

- paper cutter

- stapler and staples

Preparation

Make enough copies of pages 43–69 so that each child will be able to have his or her own dictionary. Assemble the dictionaries by putting the pages for each book in order and stapling them on the left side.

Instructions

When you begin using your word wall in class, distribute a dictionary to each child. As you add words to the word wall, have the students write them in their dictionaries on the appropriate pages. You may give them some extra words that they could use for their writing as well. You can incorporate lessons on alphabetizing, guide words, and other language skills while using these dictionaries.

Cleanup

Allow the students to store their dictionaries in their desks for reference.

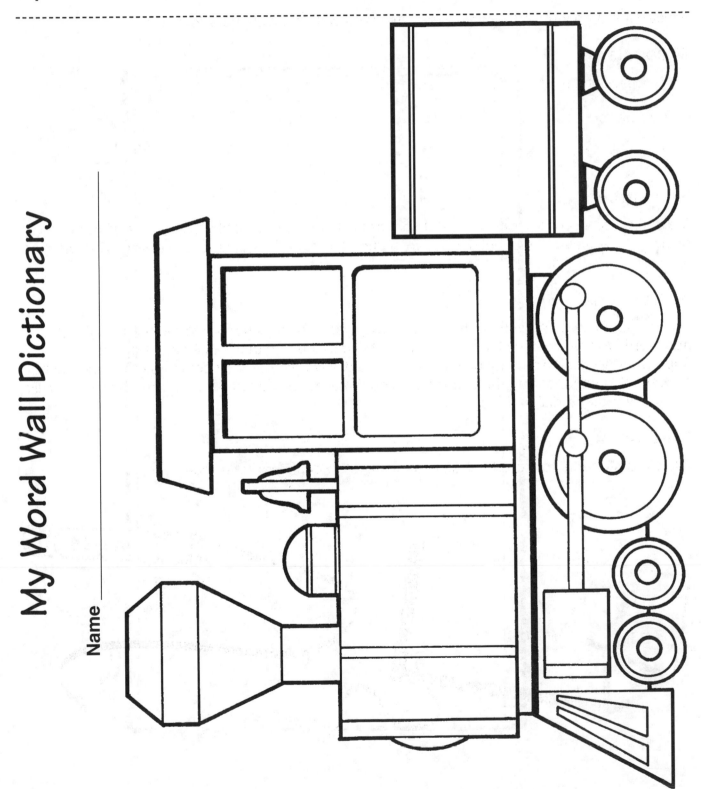
Alphabet Train

My Word Wall Dictionary

Name _____

Word Wall Dictionary (cont.)

Alphabet Train (cont.)

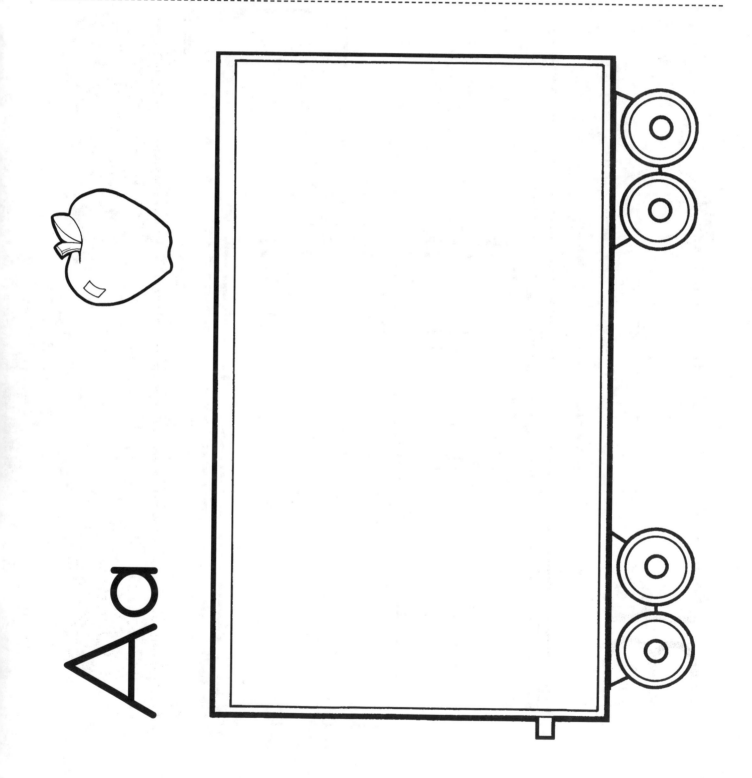

Alphabet Train *(cont.)*

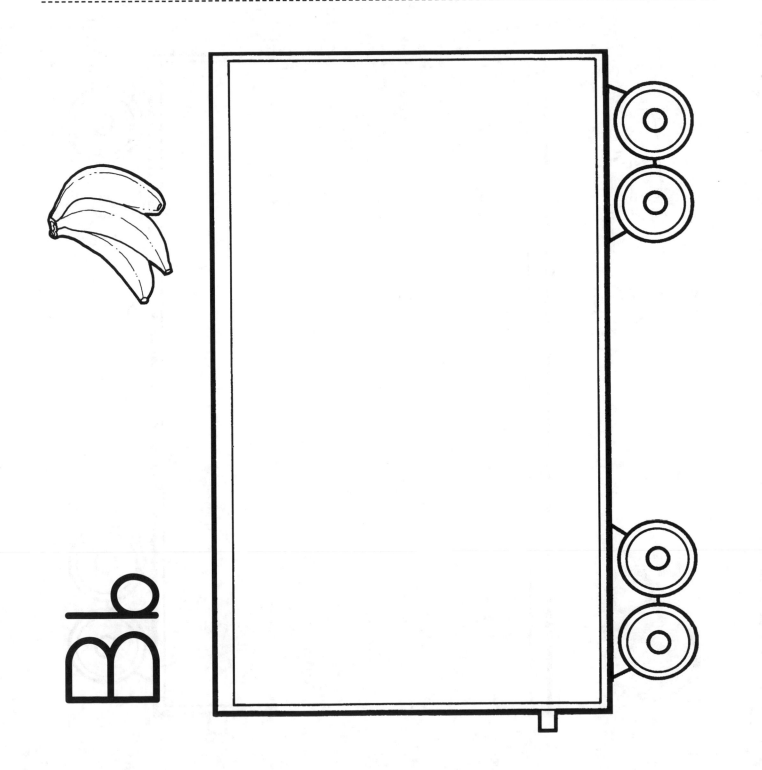

Word Wall Dictionary (cont.)

Alphabet Train (cont.)

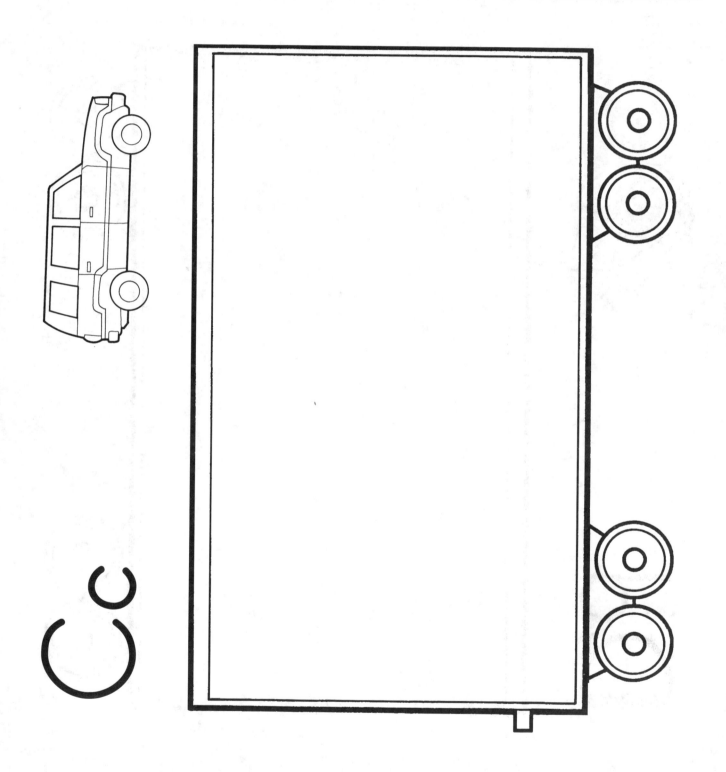

Alphabet Train *(cont.)*

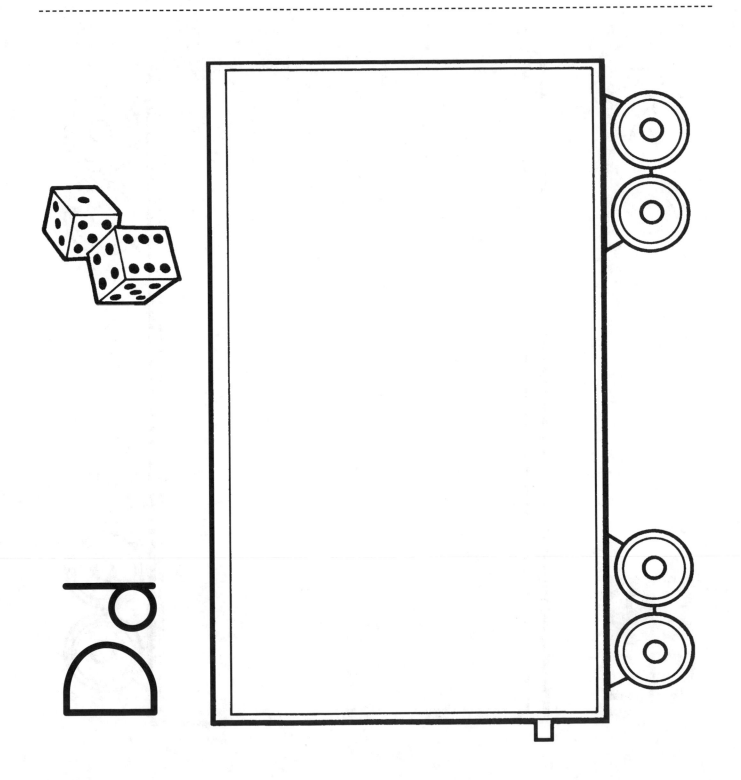

Alphabet Train *(cont.)*

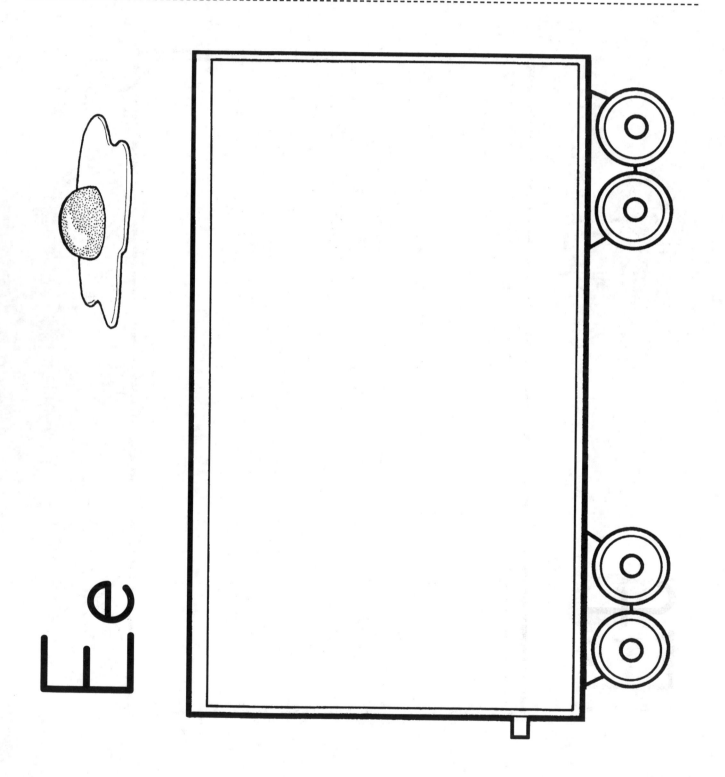

Word Wall Dictionary *(cont.)*

Alphabet Train *(cont.)*

Alphabet Train (cont.)

Alphabet Train (cont.)

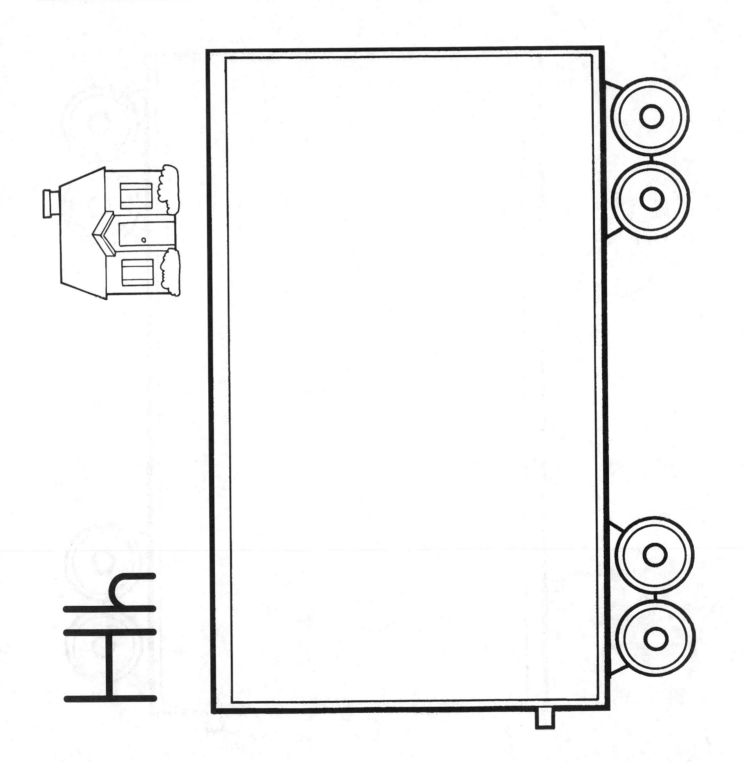

Word Wall Dictionary (cont.)

Alphabet Train (cont.)

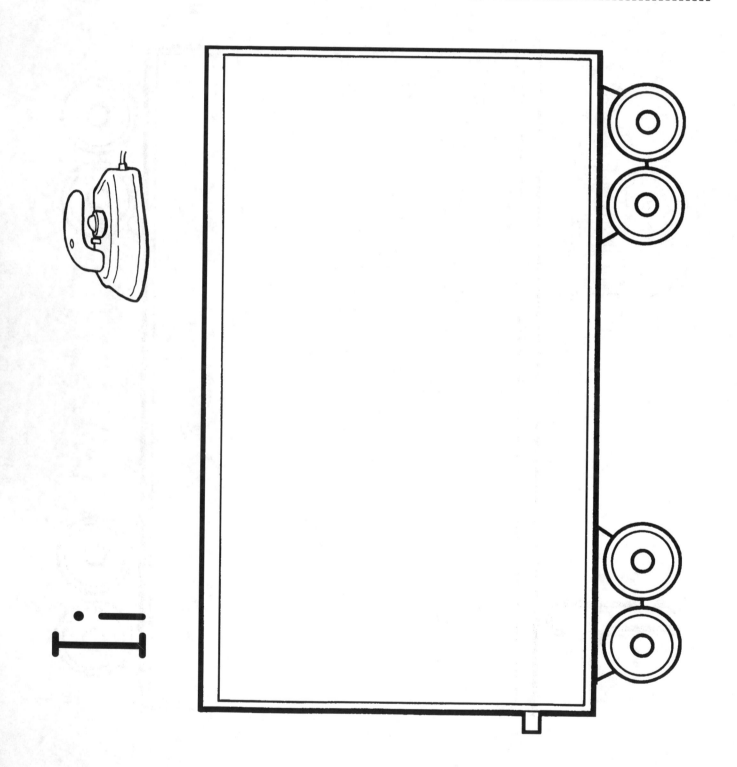

Alphabet Train (cont.)

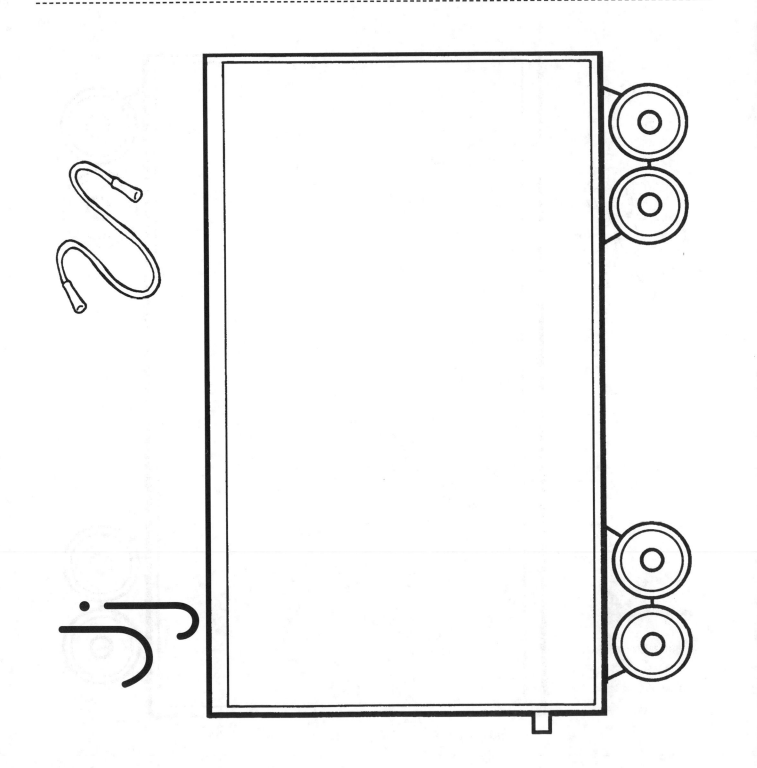

Word Wall Dictionary (cont.)

Alphabet Train (cont.)

Alphabet Train *(cont.)*

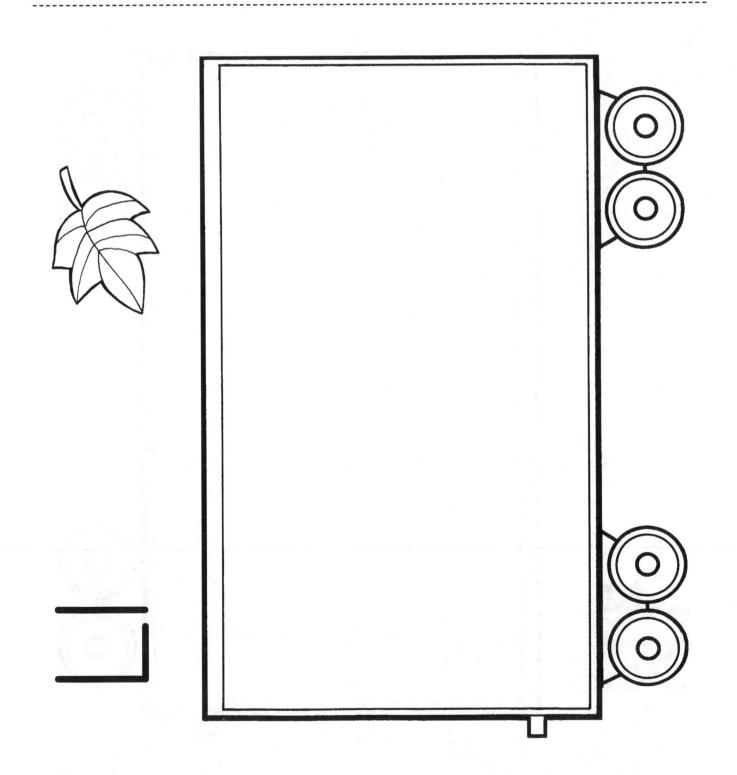

Alphabet Train *(cont.)*

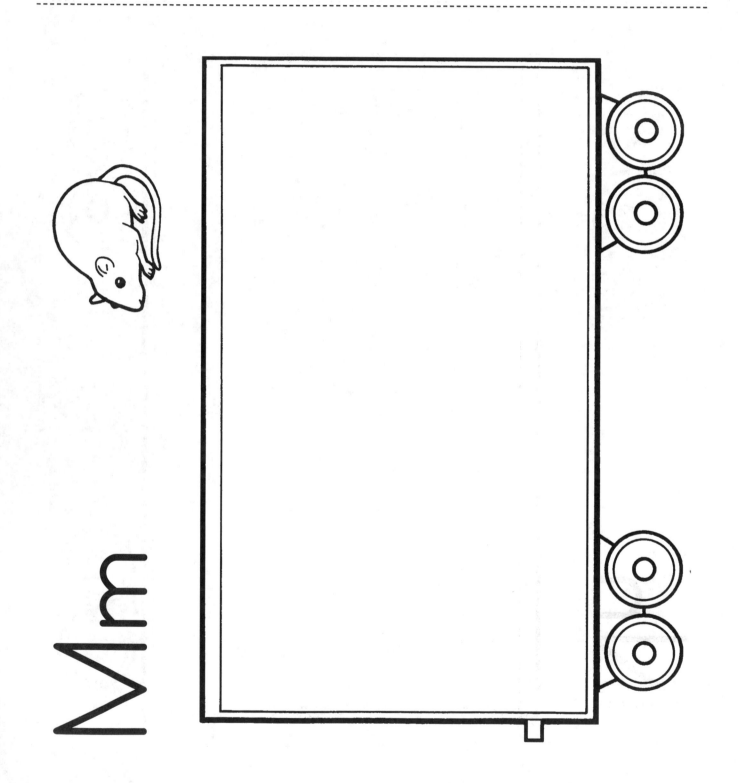

Alphabet Train *(cont.)*

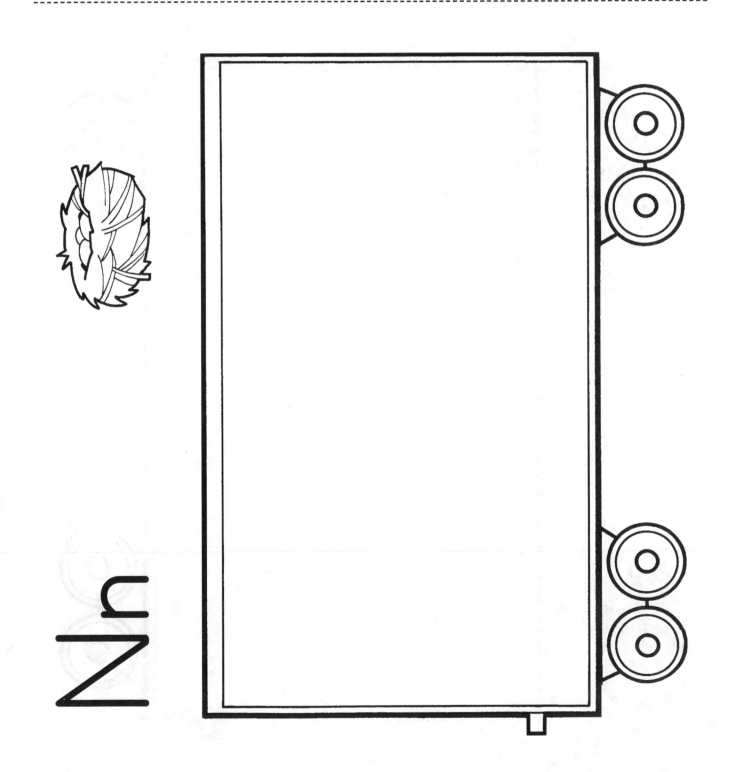

Alphabet Train *(cont.)*

Alphabet Train (cont.)

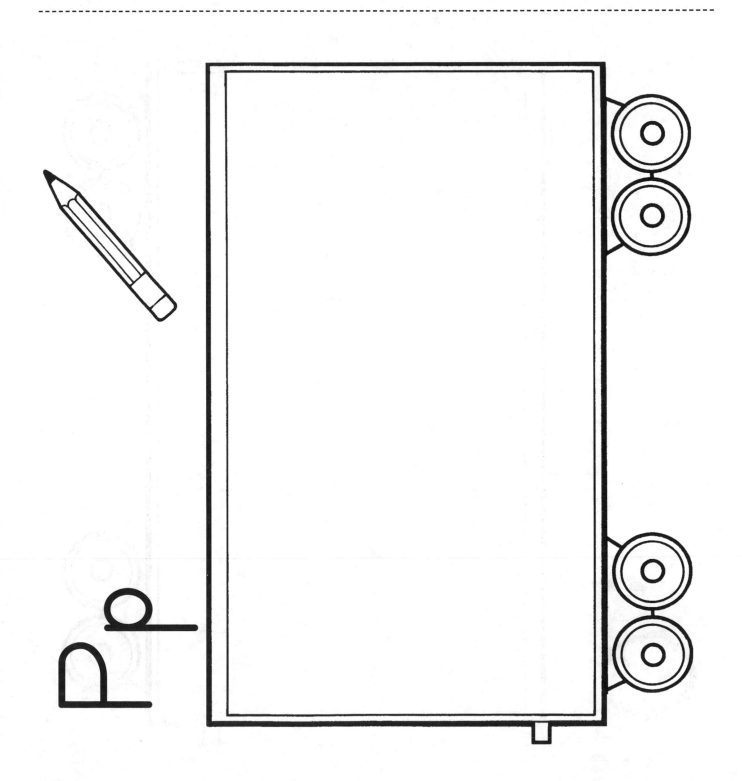

Pp

Alphabet Train (cont.)

Alphabet Train (cont.)

Alphabet Train *(cont.)*

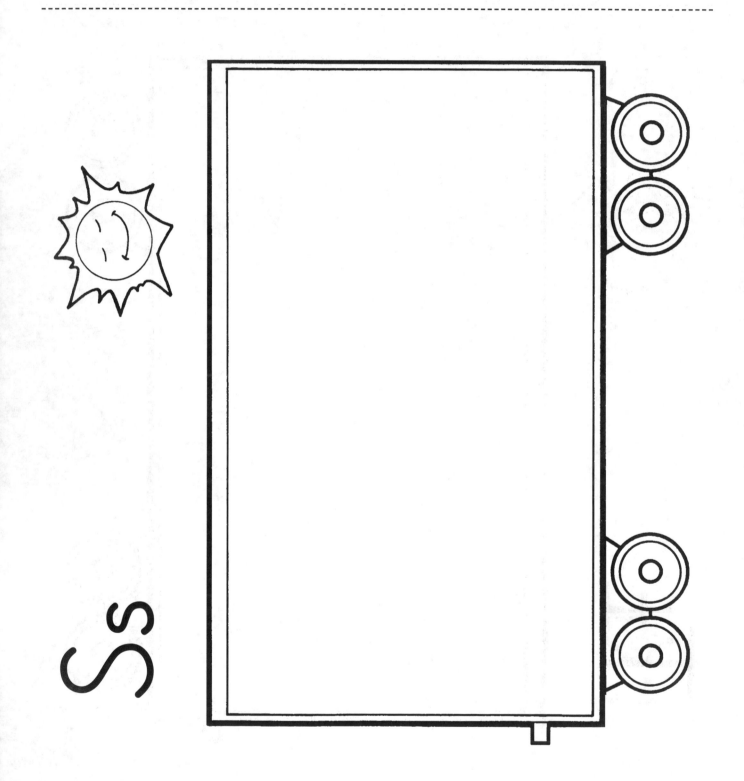

Ss

Alphabet Train *(cont.)*

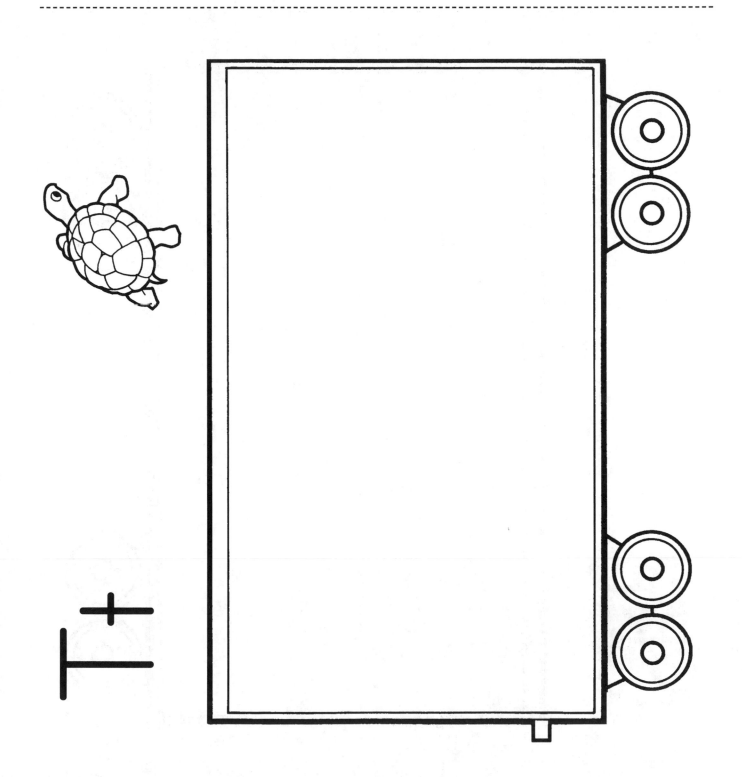

Word Wall Dictionary *(cont.)*

Alphabet Train *(cont.)*

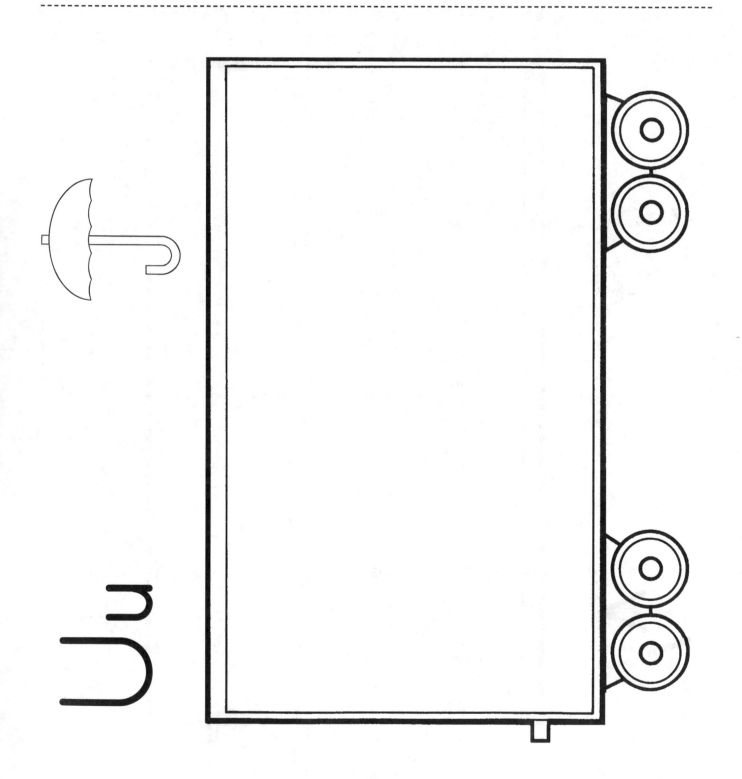

64

Alphabet Train (cont.)

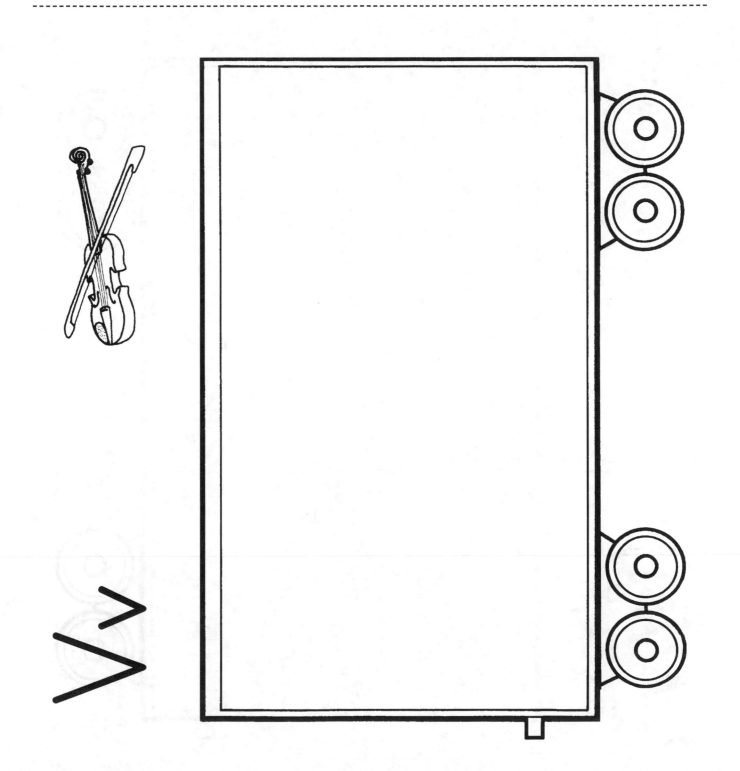

Alphabet Train (cont.)

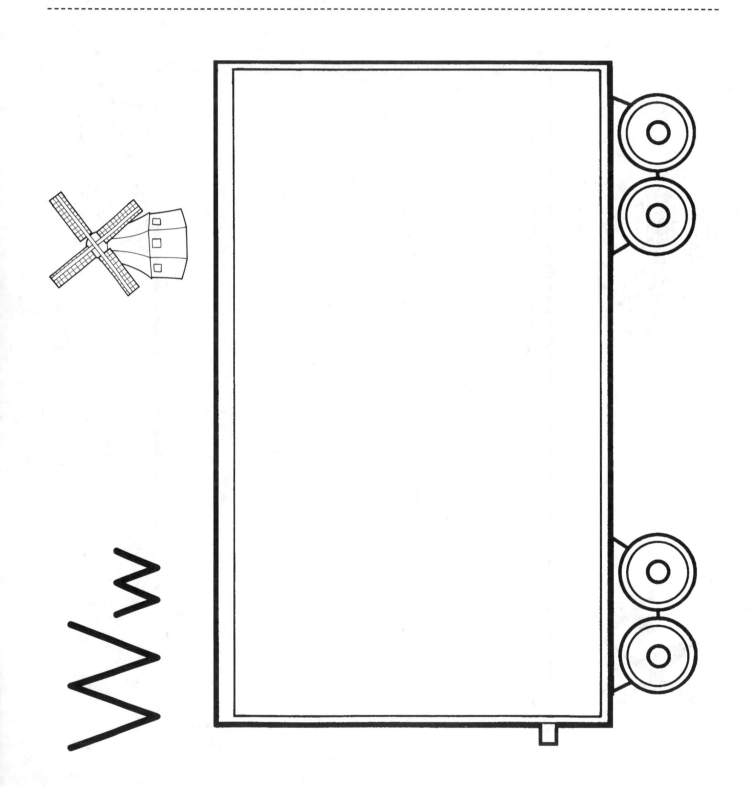

Alphabet Train *(cont.)*

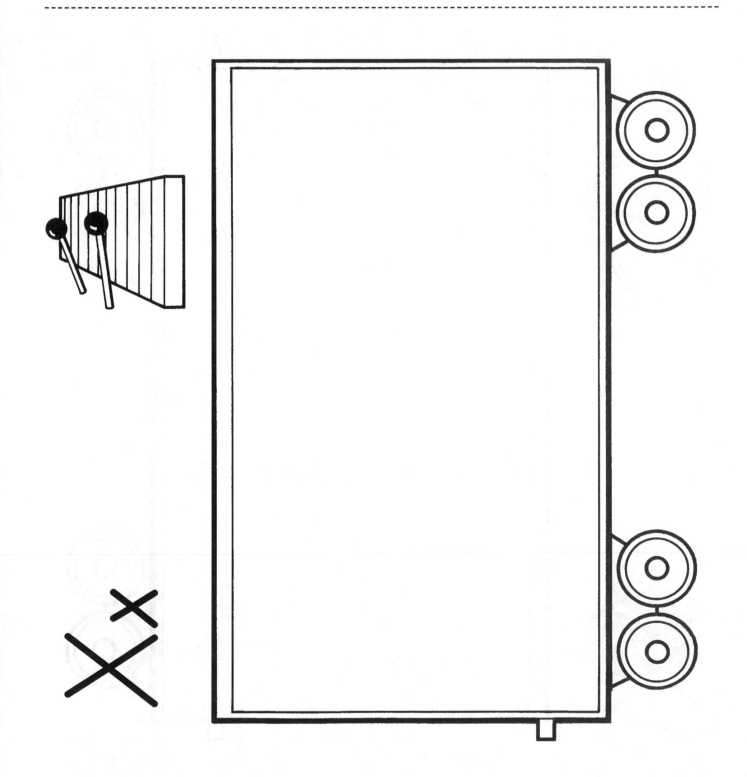

Word Wall Dictionary (cont.)

Alphabet Train (cont.)

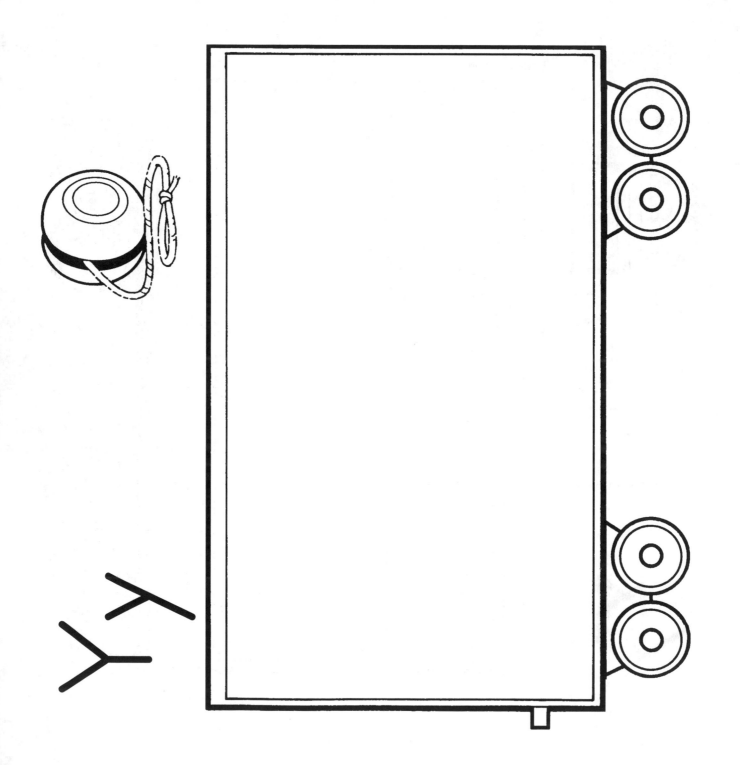

Alphabet Train (cont.)

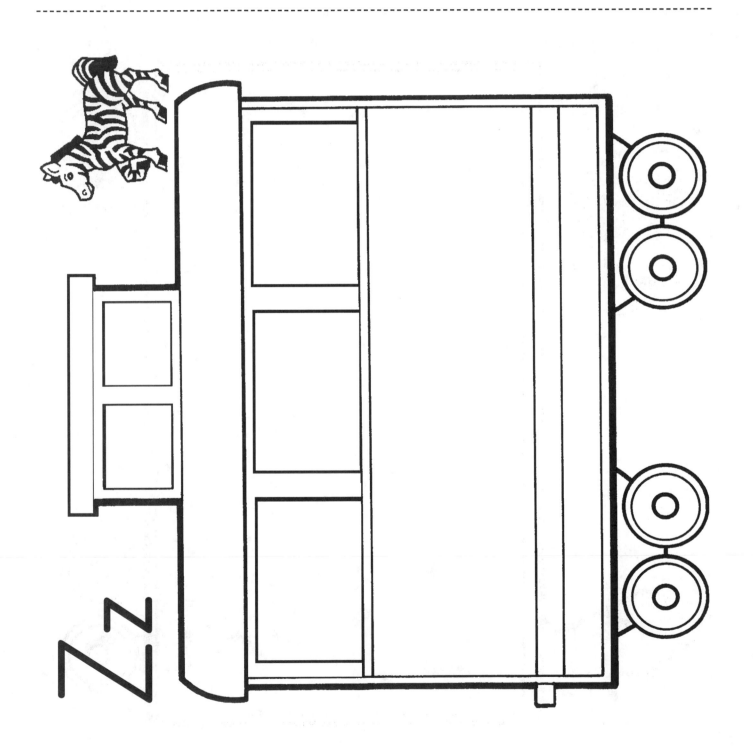

Alphabetizing Relay

Purpose

Students will alphabetize the words from the word wall.

Materials

- index cards

- markers

Preparation

The students will be divided into teams of four or five for this activity. Write the word wall words on index cards. Make a set for each group.

Instructions

Divide the students into teams of four or five. Give each team a set of word wall flash cards. The teams will race to see who can alphabetize their word cards first.

Cleanup

Wrap the sets of cards with rubber bands, and store them in a plastic bag.

Variation

If you do this activity for more than one set of word wall words, combine the cards from the current and previous sets to make one large set. Have the teams alphabetize this combined set to the first, second, and third letters.

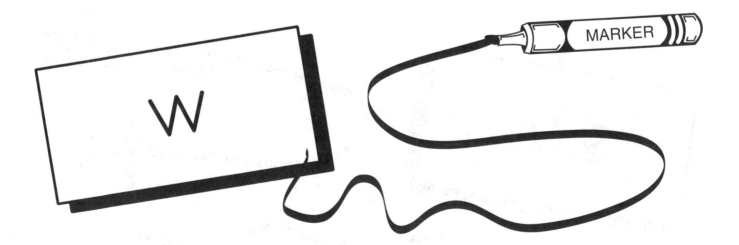

Sound Bites

Purpose

The students will use pictures to practice specific sounds.

Materials

- crayons
- magazines
- glue
- construction paper
- scissors

Preparation

Gather together a collection of old magazines.

Instructions

Choose a word from the word wall which contains a phoneme you wish to emphasize. Ask the students to cut out pictures from magazines or draw pictures that share the same phoneme as the word. The phoneme can be in the beginning, middle, or end of the word. Have them glue the pictures on construction paper. Label the tops of their papers with the phoneme that they are working on.

Cleanup

Display the pictures, and return the materials to their appropriate places.

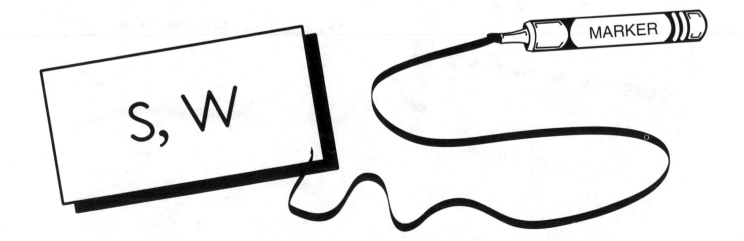

Scrambled Spelling

Purpose

The students will unscramble letters to practice spelling their word wall words.

Materials

- list of scrambled words from the word wall

- pencils

Preparation

Write down the words from the word wall in a scrambled manner. Make enough copies of the scrambled words so that every student has one.

Instructions

Hand out the scrambled words to the students. Ask them to decipher the words and to write their answers next to the scrambled words.

Cleanup

Collect the papers.

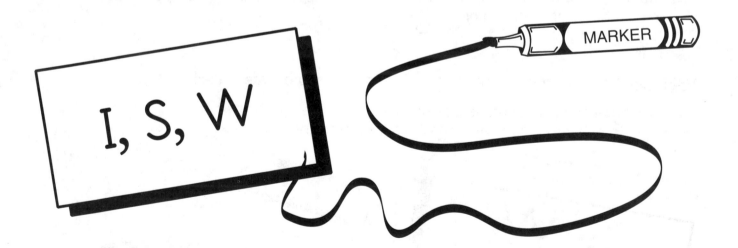

Word Wall Tic-Tac-Toe

Purpose

Students will play a game to practice reading and recognizing their word wall words.

Materials

- copies of page 74

- laminating materials

- wipe-off markers

Preparation

Write nine word wall words on the blank tic-tac-toe game board on page 74. Laminate the boards so they can be used more than once.

Instructions

Divide the students into pairs to play this tic-tac-toe game. When a student wants to mark an X or an O, he or she will need to read out loud the word in the desired square. If the player says it correctly, he or she can mark it. If the player says it incorrectly, the square stays blank. Play then passes to the other player. The game continues until someone has three Xs or Os in a row vertically, horizontally, or diagonally.

Cleanup

Ask the students to wipe off their boards. Collect the boards and markers and store them in a bag or box.

Variations

Try making several sets of game boards, each with nine different words. Let the students exchange their boards after each match so they get experience with more words.

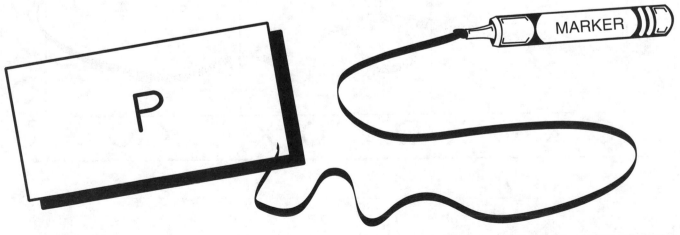

Word Wall Tic-Tac-Toe (cont.)

Tic-Tac-Toe Game Board

Sight Word Baseball

Purpose

Students will play a board game to practice reading the words from the word wall.

Materials

- copies of pages 76 and 77
- game pieces
- markers
- dice
- laminating materials

Preparation

Write some of the previous and current sight words on the baseball game board. Laminate the board if you would like to reuse it.

Instructions

Arrange the students into small groups and then divide each group into two teams. The team with the highest roll on the dice goes first. A player from the first team rolls the dice and moves his or her game piece the same amount of spaces. The player must read the word that he or she lands on and use it correctly in a sentence. If the player misses, the team has one "out." If the player answers correctly, the next player on the team comes up "to bat." The play continues until there are three "outs" on a team. An "out" is determined either by reading the word incorrectly or using it incorrectly in a sentence. Once the team has three "outs," play passes to the opposing team.

As the players pass home base, points are given. The game can continue for nine "innings" or as time permits.

Cleanup

Collect the game pieces and the game board and store them in a plastic bag.

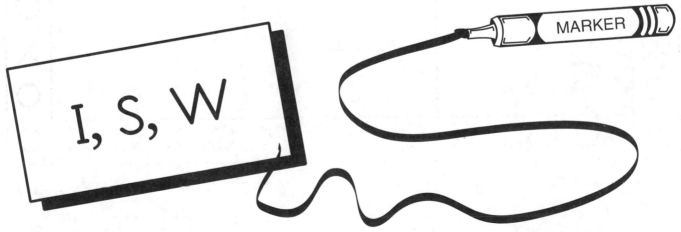

Sight Word Baseball (cont.)

Sight Word Baseball Game Board

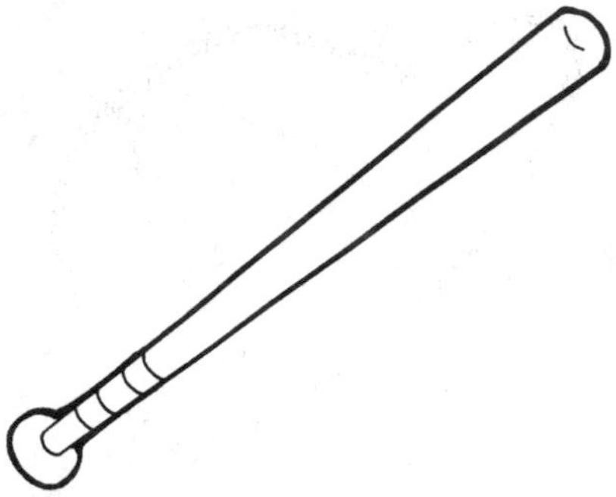

Sec

Third

Cut Here

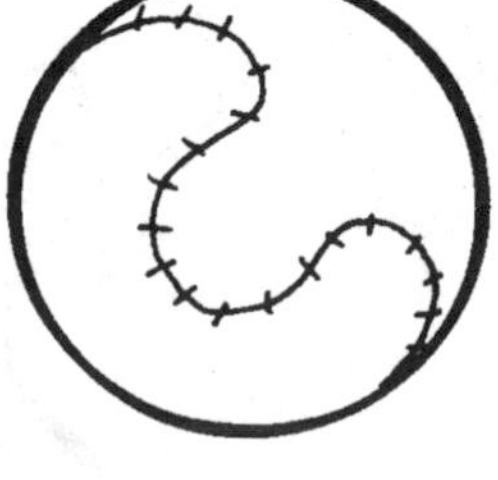

Home

Sight Word Baseball *(cont.)*

Sight Word Baseball Game Board *(cont.)*

ond

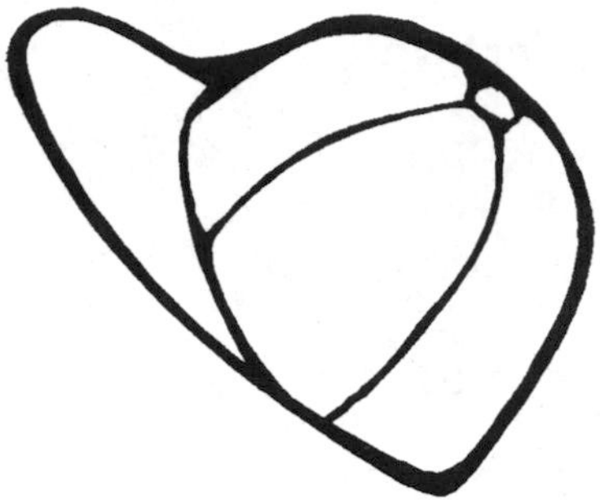

Paste Here

First

Base

⬦⬦⬦⬦⬦ACTIVITIES⬦⬦⬦⬦⬦

Sight Word Checkers

Purpose

Students will play a version of checkers to read and reinforce their word wall words.

Materials

- copies of page 79
- tape or glue
- checkers
- markers
- tagboard

Preparation

Reproduce two copies of page 79 for each pair of students. Cut and paste two half-board pieces onto a piece of tagboard to make each game board. Write the words from the word wall twice on each board, once on a blank space and once on a shaded space, until the entire game board is filled up. This will make the game even for both sides.

Instructions

The players should arrange their checkers on the board in the same way as in the traditional game. When a player wants to move his or her game piece into a new space, he or she must first read the word in that space. If the player cannot read the word correctly, he or she has to pass. If a player wishes to jump another player, he or she needs to read the word(s) in the space(s) he or she intends to land on.

The players can be "crowned" when they have reached the opposite side of the board. The game continues until one player has lost all of his or her checkers.

Cleanup

Collect the game boards and checkers. Store each set in a separate manila envelope.

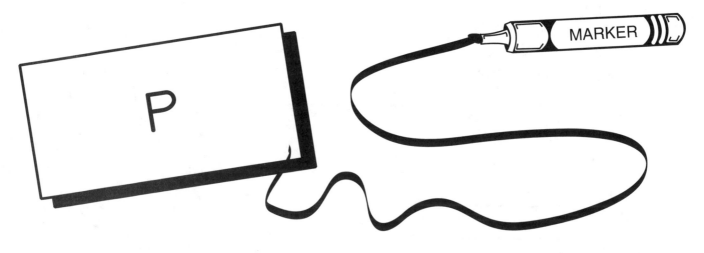

Sight Word Checkers *(cont.)*

Sight Word Checkers Game Board

This is only half of a checkerboard. Make two copies, and tape them together to make a full board. Then mount the checkerboard on tagboard for sturdiness.

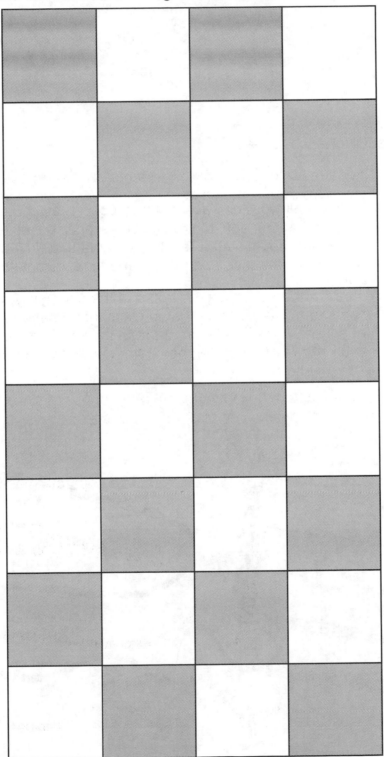

Word Puzzles

Purpose

Students will use puzzles to practice reading words from the word wall.

Materials

- copies of page 81

- markers

Preparation

Make a copy of page 81 for each student.

Instructions

Ask the students to write one wall word on each puzzle piece. They should use markers and write in very large letters. Ask the students to then color the puzzle pieces, cut them apart, and put each set of pieces in individual bags. Tell the students to switch their puzzles with each other and solve them. Have them do one puzzle at a time, completing as many as possible in the available time.

Cleanup

Store each set of puzzle pieces in a separate bag.

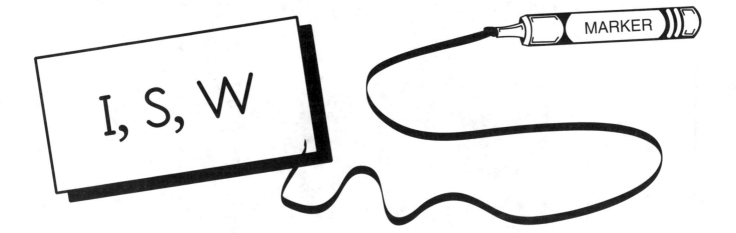

Word Puzzles (cont.)

Puzzle Pattern

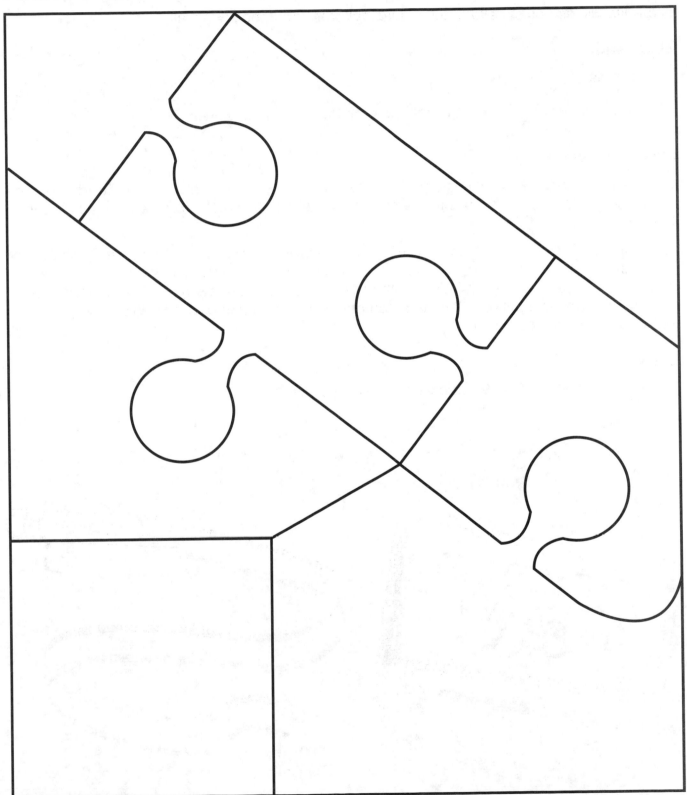

Building Crosswords

Purpose

Students will use clues to write their word wall words.

Materials

- pencils

- graph paper or crossword puzzle program (computer software)

Preparation

Use graph paper or a software program to make a crossword puzzle out of the words from the word wall. Create clues to go with the puzzle. Make a copy of the puzzle and clues for each student.

Instructions

Pass out the copies of the crossword puzzle and clues to the students. Tell the students to find the answers to the clues (they may refer to the word wall) and write them in the appropriate places.

Cleanup

Collect the papers, look them over, and send them home.

Variations

Challenge the students to build their own crossword puzzles and clues out of the words on the word wall.

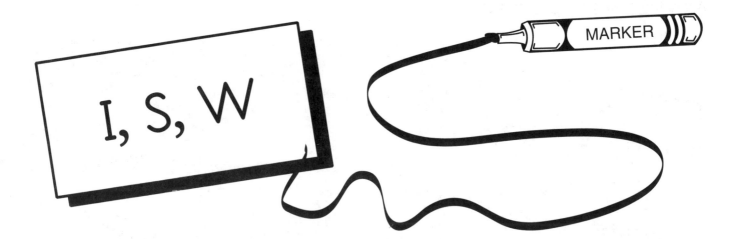

82

Cup Stackups

Purpose

Students will practice reading their word wall words in the context of sentences.

Materials

- Styrofoam or paper cups
- markers

Preparation

Think of several sentences, using as many of the word wall words as possible. Make a stack of Styrofoam or paper cups for every sentence. Each stack should have enough cups for all the words being used in the sentence. At the upper rim of each cup, write one word from the sentence so that when the cups are correctly stacked, they will form the sentence. On the insides of the cups, write their order numbers so that the children can self-correct their stacking sentences by looking inside. Randomly stack the cups and place each set in a separate bag.

Instructions

Give out a set of cups to each student. The students will spread out all of their cups and survey them. Tell them to try stacking the cups to find the correct order of the scrambled sentences. If the students want to see if their sentences are correct, they may flip the cups and read the order numbers on the insides. Once a student has solved a sentence, he or she should scramble the cups and trade them with someone else.

Cleanup

Store each set of cups in a bag. Be sure that their orders are scrambled.

Variation

Allow the students to make up their own sentences on cups.

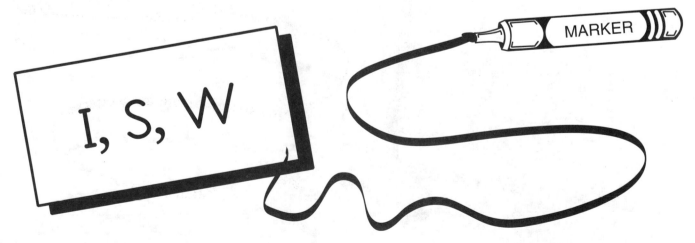

Word Card Sentences

Purpose

Students will practice reading their word wall words in the context of sentences.

Materials

- blank sentence strips or construction paper
- index cards
- envelopes
- markers
- glue
- scissors
- copies of pages 85 and 86 (optional)

Preparation

Think of several sentences, using as many of the word wall words as possible. Write the sentences on sentence strips or construction paper, or you may use the prepared sentence strips on pages 85 and 86. (These strips may not be filled with the words currently displayed on your word wall, but they are made up of some basic sight words which the students should practice.) Cut the sentences apart between each word. Glue each word onto an index card. Number the back of each index card in the order it appears in the sentence. The students can later use these numbers to check their work. Put all of the word cards for each sentence in an envelope. (**Note:** You may wish to create a system of identification so that if a card is separated from its envelope, students can figure out where it belongs.)

Instructions

Give each student a set of cards in an envelope. Each student will spread out all of his or her words and survey them. He or she will then arrange the word cards to form a complete sentence. After the student creates the sentence, he or she can turn the cards over to check the order. When finished, the student should put the word cards back in the envelope and switch with another student.

Cleanup

Store each set of word cards in a separate envelope.

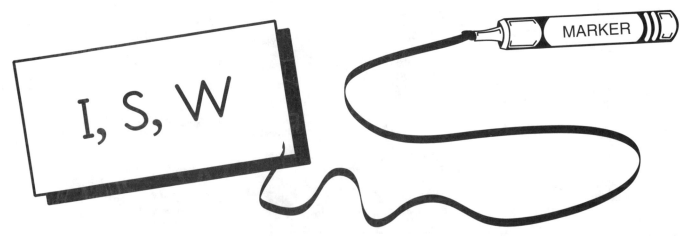

Sentence Strips

It is fun to learn about science.

We come to school each day.

At recess we play.

I like math.

Sentence Strips (cont.)

I eat lunch with my friends.

It is important to listen.

We need to cooperate.

Let's obey safety rules.

~~~~~ ACTIVITIES ~~~~~
Poetry Fun

Purpose

Students will reinforce their word wall words in the context of poetry.

Materials

- a collection of poetry and/or copies of pages 89–100 (or see the list on page 88)
- butcher paper, tagboard, or construction paper

- markers
- index cards
- pocket chart

Preparation

Find a poem that includes a current classroom theme, a curricular area you are studying, a season or month of the year, an approaching holiday, or anything else that is relevant to your students. (A poem for each month is included on the following pages.) Be sure to choose a poem that is simple and includes some basic sight words. Reproduce a large copy of the poem onto construction paper, butcher paper, or tagboard. Post it next to a pocket chart. Make individual cards for each word in the poem, including the title and punctuation.

Instructions

Distribute the cards equally among the students. They will then take turns building the poem in a pocket chart or on the floor next to the poem. They may refer to the complete copy of the poem and go word by word. Remind the students to only give each other hints if a word is hard to locate or decode. When the poem has been completely reconstructed, the group should read the poem in unison. As they read it aloud, they should also correct any mistakes that they come across.

Cleanup

Collect all of the index cards and store them in a manila envelope.

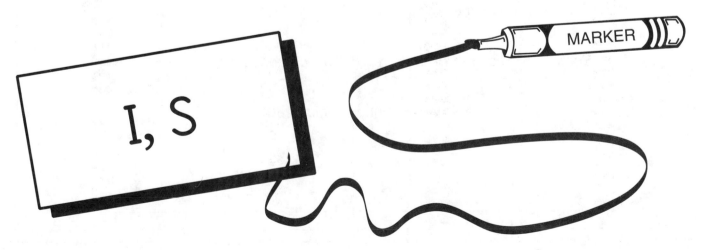

Poetry Fun (cont.)

Variations

As time permits, students can shuffle the cards and rebuild the poem, or they may use the completed poem to find word wall words, rhyming words, spelling patterns, nouns, verbs, adjectives, etc.

The following is a list of poetry resource books to get you started.

• Bennett, J. *Tiny Tim*. (Delacorte, 1982)

• dePaola, T. *Tomie dePaola's Mother Goose*. (Putnam, 1985)

• de Regniers, B., B. Schenk, M. White, and J. Bennett. *Sing a Song of Popcorn*. (Scholastic, 1988)

• Hopkins, L. B. *Surprises*. (HarperCollins, 1986)

———· *The Sky is Full of Song*. (HarperCollins, 1987)

• Larrick, N. *When the Dark Comes Dancing*. (Putnam, 1983)

• Oxenbury, H. *The Helen Oxenbury Nursery Story Book*. (Knopf, 1985)

• Prelutsky, J. *The Random House Book of Poetry for Children*. (Random House, 1983)

———· *Read Aloud Rhymes for the Very Young*. (Knopf, 1986)

———· *Something Big Has Been Here*. (Greenwillow, 1990)

• Silverstein, S. *Where the Sidewalk Ends*. (Dell, 1986)

Poetry Fun *(cont.)*

January Poem

What Can You Do with a Mitten?
Oh, there are many things!
You can use it in your garden,
Or you can make some wings.
You can dust the chairs and tables,
Or you can mop the floor.
You can make a funny puppet
Or hang it on the door.
You can use it as a washcloth
Or for your dolly's hat.
You can hang it on a flagpole
Or give it to your cat.
You can use it in the birdcage
Or for your ears of corn.
You can put it with your treasures,
And, oh!—It keeps you warm!

Poetry Fun (cont.)

February Poem

The Groundhog and His Shadow

The groundhog looks upon the ground,
Sees his shadow and goes back down.

But if he sees no shadow there
He knows it's time to leave his lair.

If shadows come, then winter lasts.
If shadows fade, then winter's past.

90

Poetry Fun (cont.)

March Poem

Poor Mr. Leprechaun

Hello there, Mr. Leprechaun.

May I ask how you have been?

Aren't you feeling very well?

You look mighty green and thin.

What, Mr. Leprechaun?

Oh, really? You don't say!

Excuse my silly question—

You're supposed to look that way!

Poetry Fun *(cont.)*

April Poem

Raindrops

Raindrops, raindrops,

Falling down.

I can see them

Touch the ground.

I can see them

Make plants grow.

Raindrops, raindrops,

Watch them flow.

92

Poetry Fun *(cont.)*

May Poem

It's May Day!

It's May Day! It's May Day!
May Day is here!
The flowers are blooming,
It's spring, my dear!
Come see the flowers,
Come hear the bees,
Spread out a picnic
Under the trees.
It's May Day! It's May Day!
May Day is here!
It's time to be happy,
Time for good cheer!

Poetry Fun (cont.)

June Poem

Summer's A Comin'

Summer's comin',
School is near an end.
Packing and goodbye-ing,
Hugging and crying,
Spending time with friends.

Summer's a comin',
Bringing fun around.
Swinging and jumping,
Twirling and hopping,
Climbing up and down.

Summer's a comin',
Bringing fun around.
Splashing and laughing,
Running and skipping,
Dancing all around.

Poetry Fun *(cont.)*

July Poem

A Lazy Summer Day

We're sitting on the porch swing
Swinging back and forth,
And watching as the birds pass
On their way back North.

There's Grandpa in the backyard,
Watering the lawn.
Grandma's sipping lemonade
In between the yawns.

Poetry Fun *(cont.)*

August Poem

August Dreams

Sleep now, all you children,
The sun's gone off to bed.
When you arise tomorrow,
New adventures lie ahead.

Poetry Fun *(cont.)*

September Poem

What Makes a Grandparent?

What makes a grandparent?
It's easy to tell.
But it's not glasses
Or a cookie smell.

It's not a garden
Or silvery hair.
It's not fishing poles
Or a rocking chair.

What makes a grandparent?
You probably know.
Loving a grandchild
Is what makes one so.

Poetry Fun (cont.)

October Poem

Autumn Fun

When leaves of green turn red and brown,
And one by one come tumbling down.
When a frosty chill fills the air,
Then autumn days, we know, are here.

So take your sweater, coat, and hat,
And bundle up with this and that.
Don't worry if the cold comes in,
Just let the autumn fun begin!

Poetry Fun *(cont.)*

November Poem

Five Little Turkeys

(Traditional)

Five little turkeys standing in a row. *(Hold up five fingers.)*
First little turkey said, "I don't want to grow." *(Wiggle thumb.)*
Second little turkey said, "Why do you say that?" *(Wiggle first finger.)*
Third little turkey said, "I want to get fat." *(Wiggle next finger.)*
Fourth little turkey said, "Thanksgiving is near." *(Wiggle next finger.)*
Fifth little turkey said, "Yes, that's what I hear." *(Wiggle next finger.)*
Then the five little turkeys that were standing in a row
All said together, "Come on, let's go!" *(Run fingers away.)*

Ten Fat Turkeys

(Traditional)

Ten fat turkeys standing in a row. *(Hold up 10 fingers.)*
They spread their wings and tails just so. *(Fan out fingers.)*
They strut to the left. *(Fingers go left.)*
They strut to the right. *(Fingers go right.)*
They all stand up, ready to fight. *(Fingers are still and straight.)*
Along comes a man, he was just one. *(Hold up one finger.)*
Gobble, gobble, gobble—just watch him run! *(Make fingers wiggle.)*.

Poetry Fun *(cont.)*

December Poem

Winter World
Ice on the pond,
Snow on the trees,
Frost on the glass,
Icicles freeze.

Glistening sky,
Air crisp and clear,
Winter-white world,
Jack Frost was here.

☆☐☆☐☐A☐C☐T☐I☐V☐I☐T☐I☐E☐S☐☐☆☐☐☐

Minibooks

Purpose

Students will practice reading sight words and their word wall words in the context of a story.

Materials

- copies of pages 102–106 or blank paper

- scissors

- stapler and staples

- crayons or colored pencils

Preparation

Photocopy a set of pages 102–106 for each student. This minibook has some basic sight words for your students to practice. If you would rather concentrate on your current word wall words, cut half sheets of blank paper for the students to write their own stories.

Instructions

The students will color, cut, assemble, and read their mini books. If they are making their own books, have them pick their topics, write their stories, then edit, publish, and illustrate them. In either case, have students identify or highlight any words that are difficult for them.

Cleanup

The minibooks can be stored at home or in the students' desks.

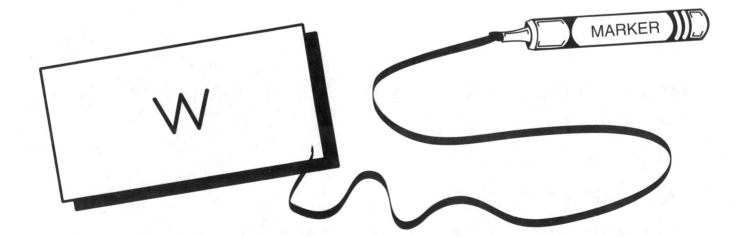

Minibooks *(cont.)*

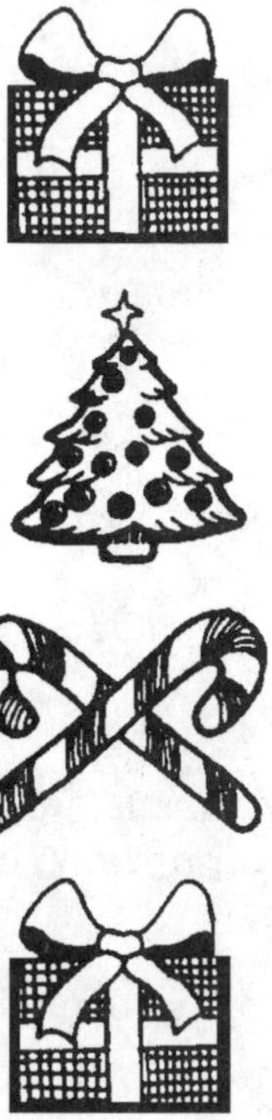

My Little Book

of

Is It Christmas Yet?

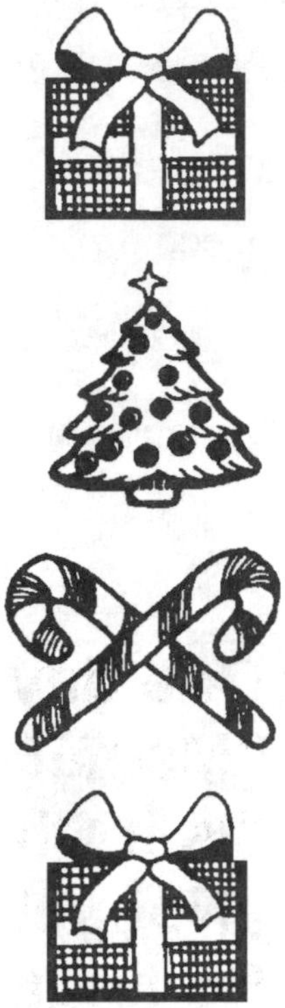

____

Name

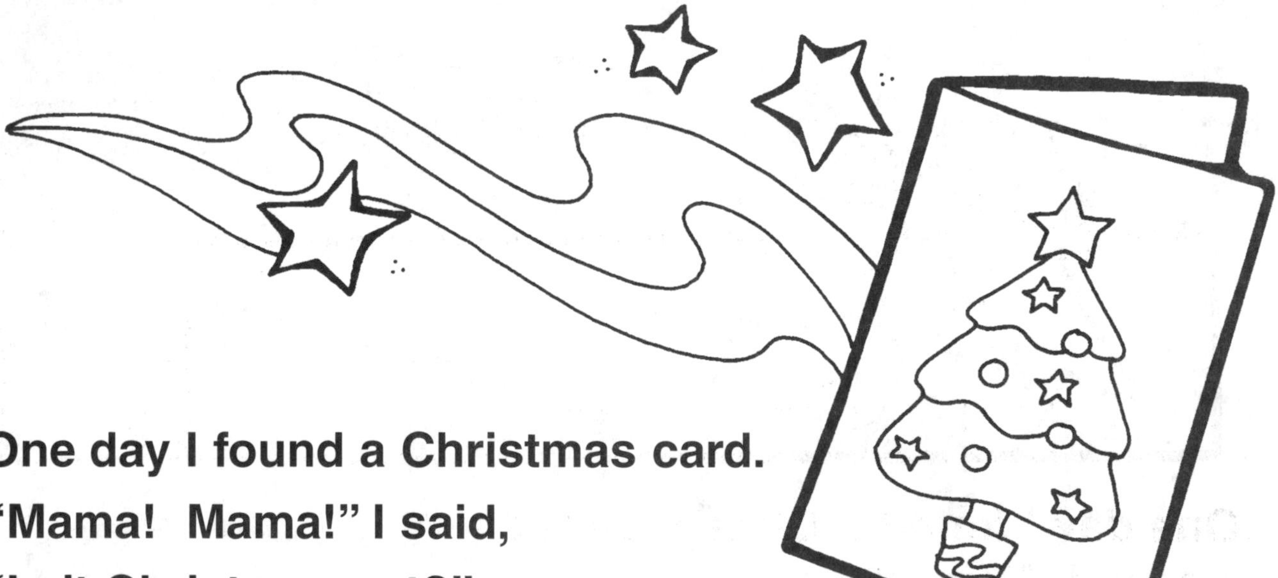

One day I found a Christmas card.
"Mama! Mama!" I said,
"Is it Christmas yet?"
"Not yet," said Mama.
So I put it in the closet, and I waited.

1

Minibooks (cont.)

One day I found a candy cane.
"Mama! Mama!" I said,
"Is it Christmas yet?"
"Not yet," said Mama.
So I put it in the closet, and I waited.

2

One day I found a Christmas present.
"Mama! Mama!" I said,
"Is it Christmas yet?"
"Not yet," said Mama.
So I put it in the closet, and I waited.

3

One day I found a Christmas tree.
"Mama! Mama!" I said,
"Is it Christmas yet?"
"Not yet," said Mama.
So I put it in the closet, and I waited.

4

One day I found a reindeer.
"Mama! Mama!" I said,
"Is it Christmas yet?"
"Not yet," said Mama.
So I put him in the closet, and I waited.

5

One day I found an elf.
"Mama! Mama!" I said,
"Is it Christmas yet?"
"Not yet," said Mama.
So I put him in the closet, and I waited.

6

One day I found Santa!
"Mama! Mama!" I said,
"Is it Christmas yet?"
"Yes," said Mama.

7

Minibooks *(cont.)*

Out came the Christmas card.
Out came the candy cane.
Out came the Christmas present.
Out came the Christmas tree.
Out came the reindeer.
Out came the elf.

8

"Ho, ho, ho!" said Santa,
and it was Christmas!

9

Create a Word

Purpose

Create word wall words using alphabet letters.

Materials

- back-to-back copies of pages 108–117 (See below for copying directions.)
- storage containers (tackle boxes, photo boxes, file card boxes, etc.)
- resealable plastic bags
- laminating materials
- pocket chart

Preparation

Make several, two-sided copies of pages 108–117 on fairly thick paper or cardstock so that the letters do not show through. Carefully arrange the letters so that each uppercase letter has its lowercase partner copied on the flip side of the paper. You may want to copy the consonants on one color and the vowels on another color. Cut out the letter and laminate them. Make an enlarged set of letters (in the same way as above) for your own use.

Instructions

Choose some word wall words that you would like to reinforce. You will lead this activity by using your large alphabet letters and a pocket chart in the front of the room. Give the students clues to a word. For example, say, "I'm thinking of a word that begins with 't' and has four letters." Once the group has created the word in the pocket chart, have the students recreate it out of their letters. If you wish to work with more than one word at a time, find patterns in the words and give clues to the students to create these words. Variations for this activity include the following: You can scramble a word wall word using your large letters and then have the students try to unscramble it with their smaller letters. You also can display a word wall word with one or more letters missing and then have the students try to figure out which letters are missing.

Cleanup

Collect the letters and seal them in bags. Store the bags in a place of easy access for the students.

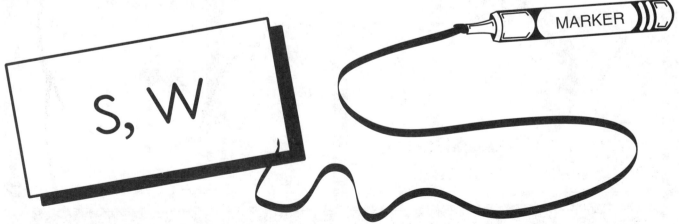

 #2481 Word Walls Activities

Create a Word (cont.)

Alphabet Cards

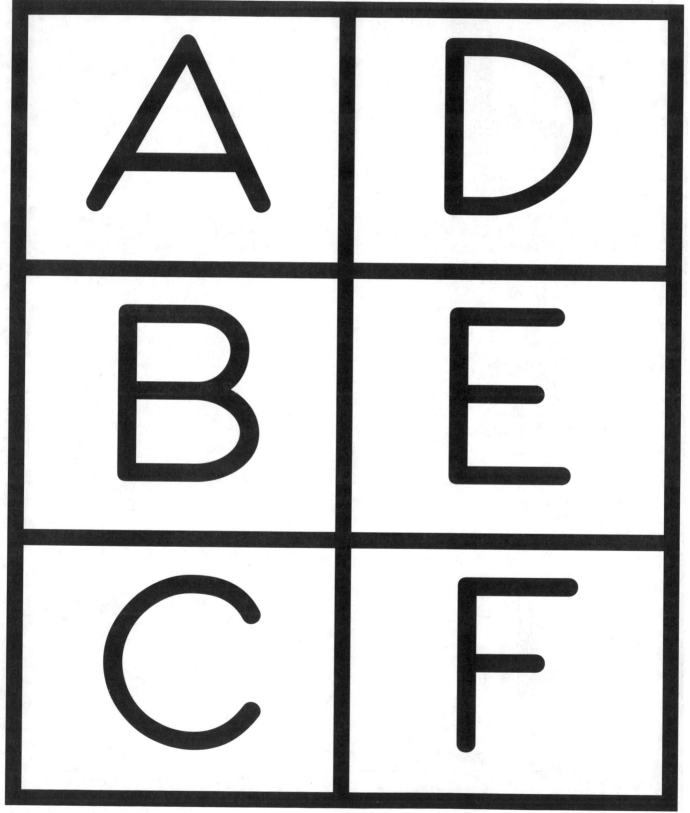

Create a Word (cont.)

Alphabet Cards (cont.)

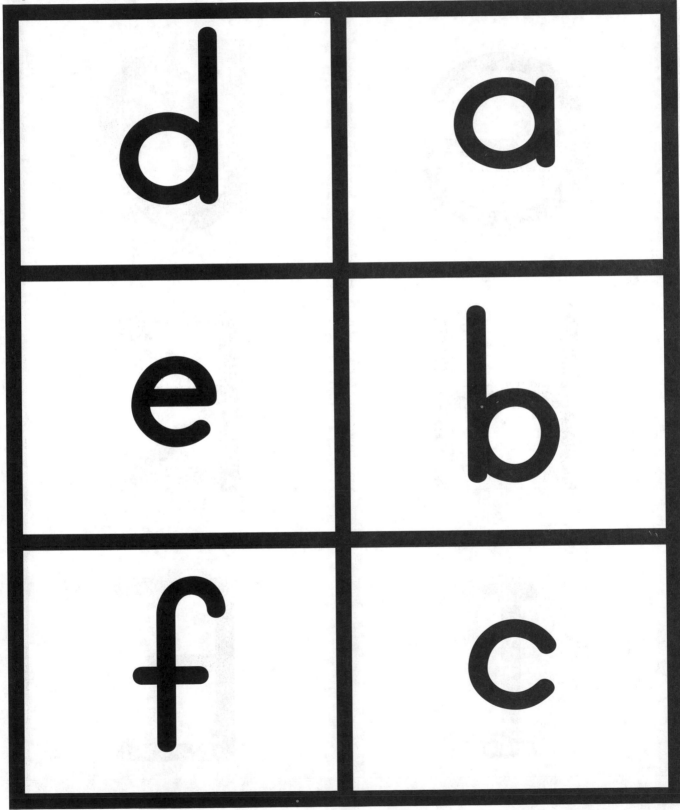

Create a Word *(cont.)*

Alphabet Cards *(cont.)*

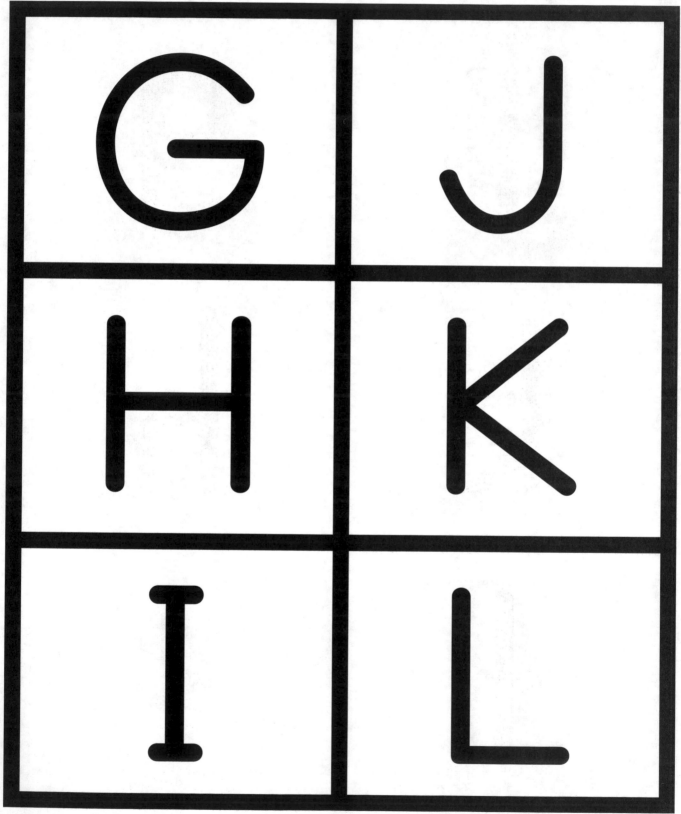

Create a Word (cont.)

Alphabet Cards (cont.)

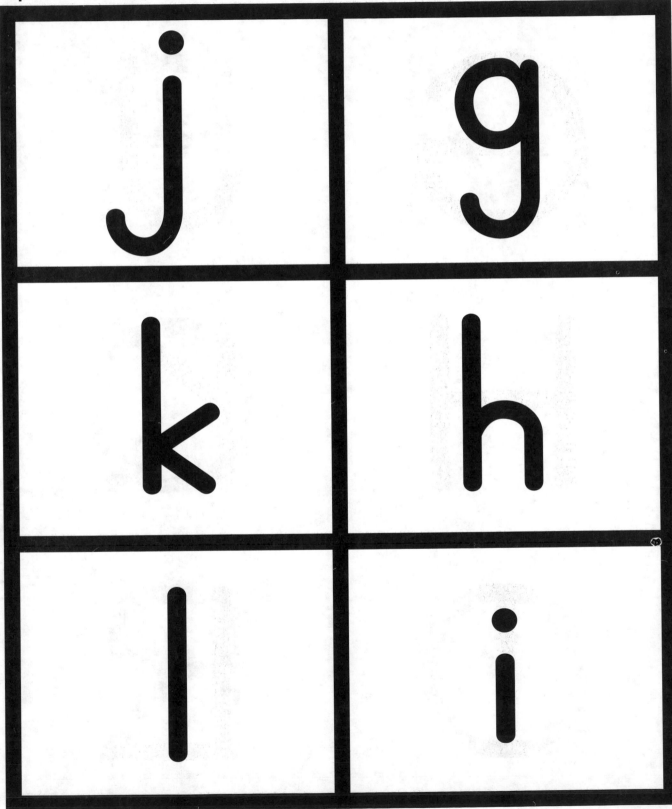

Create a Word (cont.)

Alphabet Cards (cont.)

112

Create a Word (cont.)

Alphabet Cards (cont.)

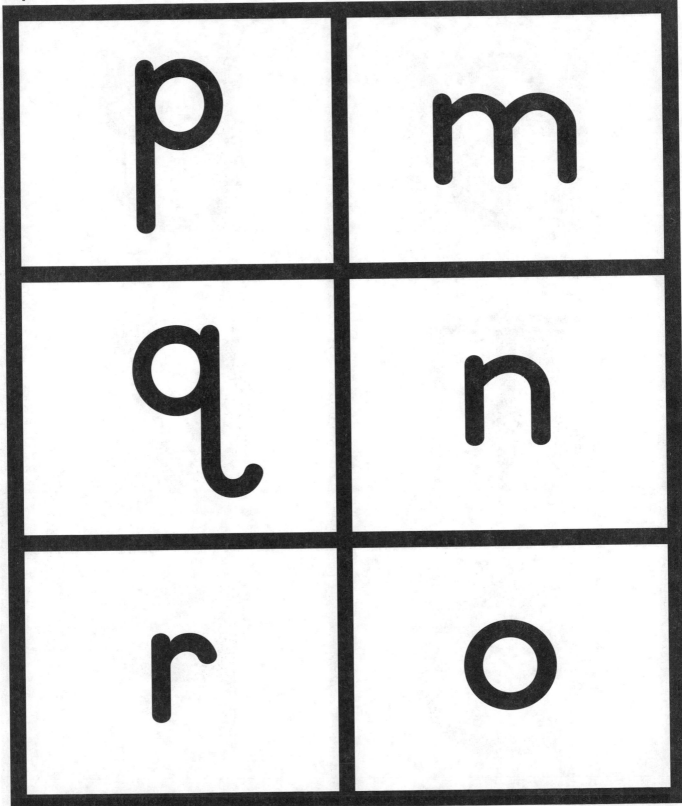

Create a Word (cont.)

Alphabet Cards (cont.)

Create a Word (cont.)

Alphabet Cards (cont.)

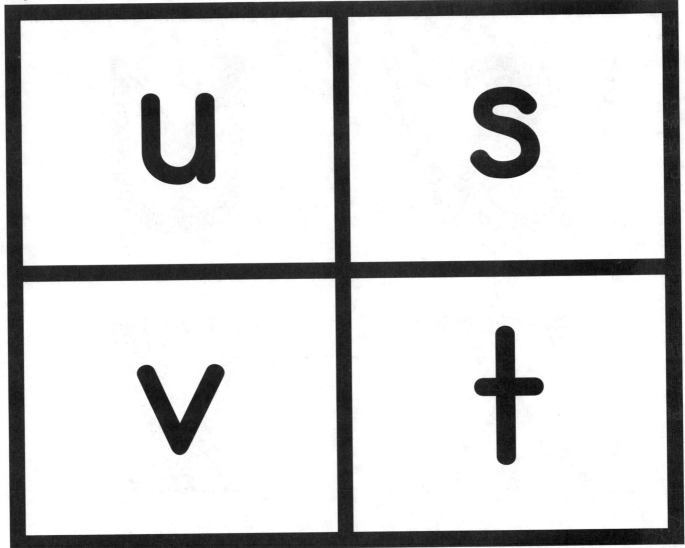

Create a Word *(cont.)*

Alphabet Cards *(cont.)*

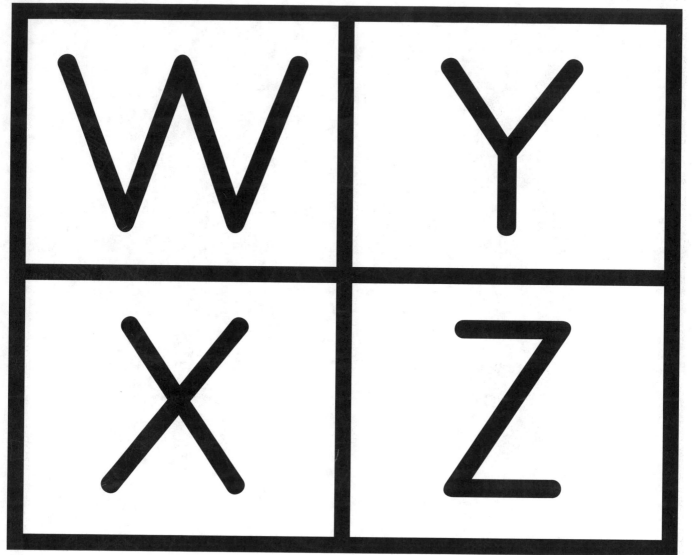

116

Create a Word *(cont.)*

Alphabet Cards *(cont.)*

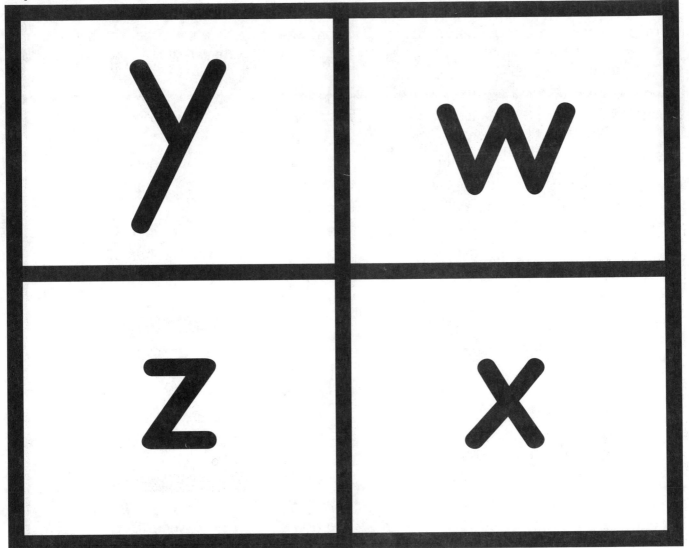

COMPOUND WORDS

Compound Words Resource List

Compound words are two or more smaller words that are put together to form a new, bigger word with a new meaning.

Compound words are a wonderful theme for a word wall. Here is a list to get you started. The following pages describe some activities for compound words, whether or not you choose to do a related word wall.

airline	buttercup	driveway	football
airplane	butterfly	drugstore	footprint
anybody	campfire	drumstick	gentleman
anyone	campground	eardrum	gingerbread
anything	cannot	earring	goldfish
anyway	cardboard	earthquake	grandfather
anywhere	catfish	eggplant	grandmother
armchair	cattail	eggshell	grapefruit
arrowhead	chalkboard	evergreen	grasshopper
artwork	clothespin	everybody	greenhouse
ballpark	cobweb	everyone	groundhog
bareback	cookbook	everything	grownup
barnyard	cookout	everywhere	hairbrush
baseball	copycat	eyeball	haircut
baseman	cornbread	eyebrow	halfway
basketball	corncob	eyelash	handshake
bathrobe	cornmeal	eyelid	headache
bathroom	cowboy	farmland	headband
bathtub	cowgirl	fingernail	headfirst
bedroom	cupboard	firecracker	headlight
bedtime	cupcake	firefighter	headline
beehive	daydream	firefly	headrest
birdbath	daylight	fireplace	headstand
birdhouse	doghouse	firewood	headstrong
birthday	doorbell	fireworks	heatstroke
blackboard	doorknob	fishbowl	highchair
bluebird	doormat	fisherman	hillside
boxcar	downhill	flagpole	homemade
breakfast	downstairs	flashlight	homework
broomstick	driftwood	flowerpot	horseback

Compound Words Resource List (cont.)

horsefly	outhouse	seesaw	taillight
horseshoe	outline	shipwreck	teacup
hourglass	outside	sidewalk	teamwork
houseboat	overall	skateboard	teapot
housewife	overcoat	smokestack	teaspoon
hubcap	overcome	snowball	textbook
indoor	overlook	snowflake	thumbtack
inside	overtime	snowman	toadstool
into	paintbrush	somebody	toothache
junkyard	pancake	someday	toothbrush
keyboard	patchwork	someone	treetop
ladybug	peanut	something	underground
lifetime	pillowcase	somewhere	underline
lighthouse	pincushion	spaceship	understand
lookout	playground	springtime	underwear
lunchroom	playhouse	stagecoach	upright
mailbox	policeman	stairway	wallpaper
mailman	popcorn	starfish	warehouse
mealtime	postman	starlight	washcloth
milkman	quarterback	steamroller	waterfall
milkshake	railroad	storybook	weekend
moonbeam	rainbow	strawberry	whatever
moonlight	raincoat	suitcase	whenever
motorboat	raindrop	sunburn	whirlwind
motorcycle	rattlesnake	Sunday	whoever
mousetrap	roadside	sundown	wildlife
necklace	rowboat	sunflower	windmill
necktie	runway	sunlight	windshield
newspaper	sailboat	sunset	wintertime
nighttime	salesman	sunshine	within
nobody	sandpaper	sweatband	without
notebook	scarecrow	sweatshirt	woodland
nothing	schoolhouse	sweetheart	worthwhile
nowhere	seafood	swordfish	yourself
outcome	seashell	tablecloth	
outdoors	seashore	tablespoon	

Compound Families

Purpose

Students will make a list of compound words which all share one "family" word.

Materials

- Compound Words Resource List (pages 118 and 119)

- paper

- pencils

Preparation

No preparation is necessary.

Instructions

The student will choose a "family" word such as *ball* and write it at the top of the paper. (Students may refer to the resource list on pages 118 and 119 for some ideas.) Then, he or she will make a list of compound words that each contain one similar part (e.g., basketball, football, baseball, ballroom, etc.). If time permits, the words can also be illustrated.

Cleanup

Collect the word lists and display them.

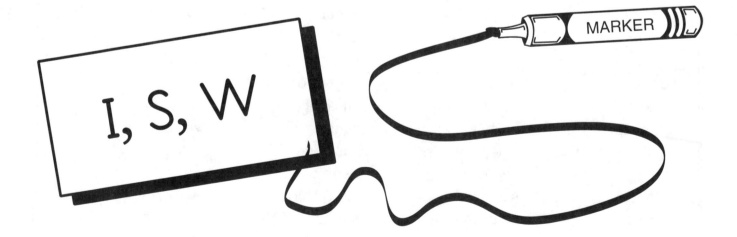

COMPOUND WORDS

Compound Creation

Purpose

Students will identify the small words that make up compound words.

Materials

- Compound Words Resource List (pages 118 and 119)
- index cards
- colored pencils or crayons
- stapler
- old magazines and scissors (optional)

Preparation

Display the word list from pages 118 and 119.

Instructions

Tell students to each choose a compound word from the list or one of their own. Ask them to write their chosen words on index cards and to draw simple pictures to represent their words. Then instruct the students to each fold a second index card in half. On this card the student should write the two words that make up his or her compound word and then illustrate the two smaller words. Allow the students to make as many cards as they can during the lesson period.

Cleanup

Staple each student's cards into a book format and label it "My Compound Word Book." Allow the students to keep their books in their desks or at home.

Variations

Instead of illustrating the books themselves, the children could cut out representative pictures from magazines and glue them to the index cards.

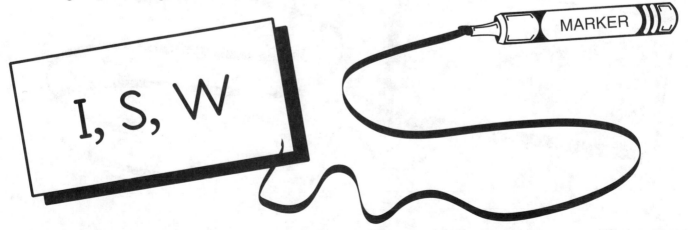

Compound Word Puzzles

Purpose

Students will be looking for the smaller words that make up compound words.

Materials

- Compound Words Resource List (pages 118 and 119)

- index cards or copies of page 123

- markers

- scissors

Preparation

On an index card, write a compound word. Leave a slight space between the two parts of the compound word. Then, cut the index card (using a unique cut) between the two small words. Make as many of these cards as you would like and laminate them. You may instead choose to use the blank patterns on page 123.

Instructions

The students will lay out the puzzle pieces and piece them together. They will know that they have made a match when they create a compound word and the cut edges fit together correctly.

Cleanup

Store the puzzle pieces in a resealable bag or in a manila envelope.

Compound Word Puzzles (cont.)

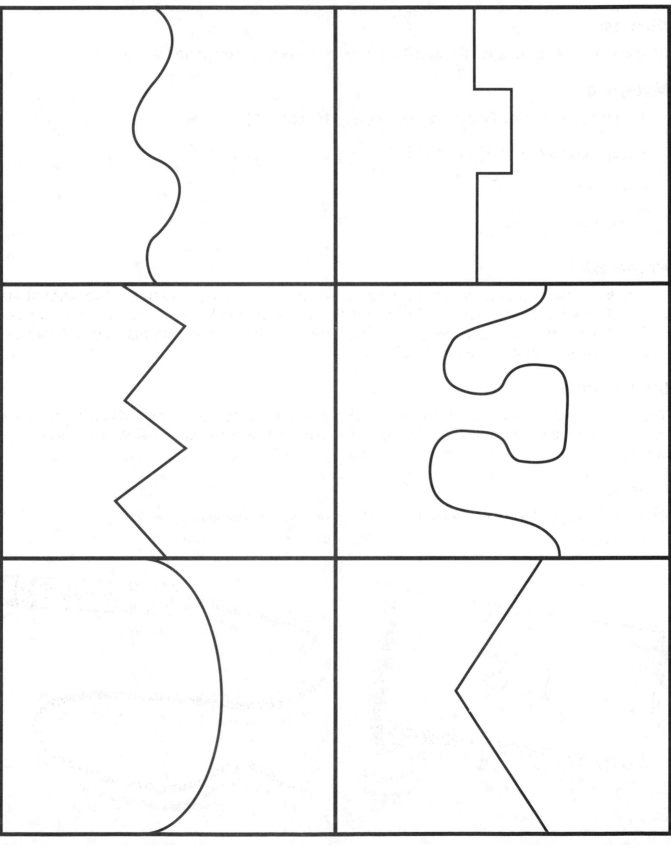

Compound Mittens

Purpose

Students will match word pairs to form compound words.

Materials

- Compound Words Resource List (pages 118 and 119)

- copies of page 125

- markers

- scissors

Preparation

Let the students prepare this activity. Give them each a pair of mittens. Each student will write the parts of a compound word on a pair of mittens. Students may come up with their own compound words or use the list provided (pages 118 and 119). After the mittens have been decorated and cut out, laminate them.

Instructions

To start this activity, the students will lay out all of the mittens on the floor. They will match two mittens together to form each correct compound word. For example, the word *cup* on one mitten would make a match with the word *cake* on another mitten. After matching all of the mittens, have the students check their compound words to see if they make sense.

Cleanup

Store the mittens in a resealable plastic bag or in a manila envelope.

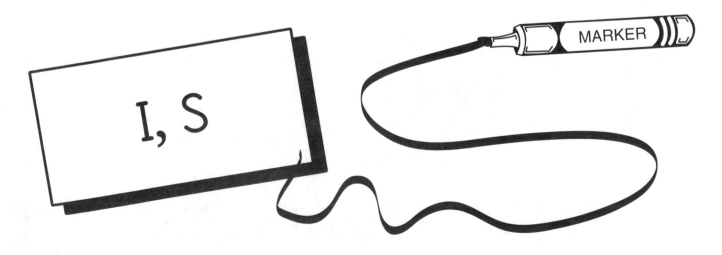

Compound Mittens *(cont.)*

Mitten Patterns

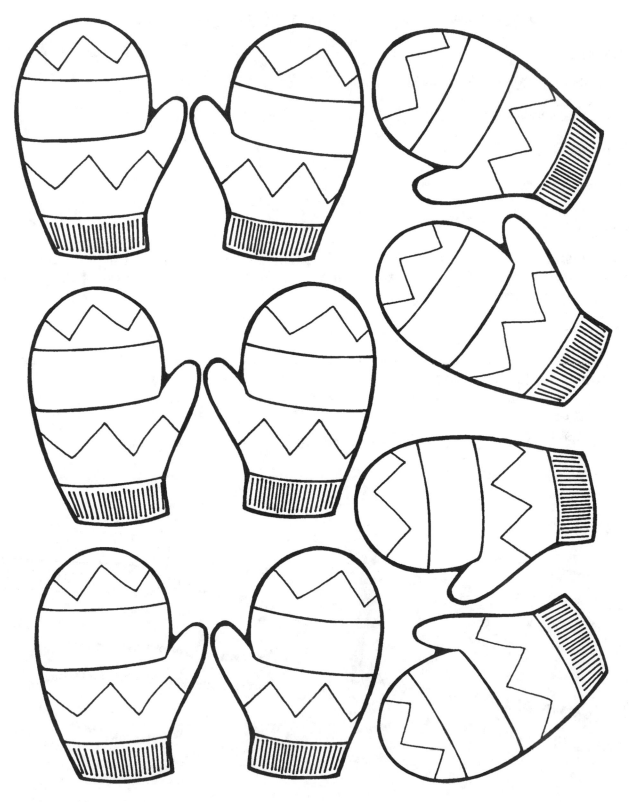

Cracked Compounds

Purpose

Students will match compound word parts together to make compound words.

Materials

- copies of pages 127 and 128

- Compound Words Resource List (pages 118 and 119)

- markers

- scissors

Preparation

Make copies of pages 127 and 128. If you would rather use your own set of compound words, use corrective fluid over the words and write in your own words before making copies. Cut out the turtle and the shell parts and laminate them.

Instructions

The students will lay out the turtle and shell pieces. They will then match the shell pieces to the turtle's back to form compound words.

Cleanup

Place each turtle and its shell pieces in a separate resealable, plastic bag.

Cracked Compounds *(cont.)*

Cracked Compounds Turtle

Directions: Help the turtle make some compound words.

1. Read the Hint.

2. Create compound words by placing each shell piece on the back of the turtle's shell.

Hint

Compound words are made from two smaller words put together to make one word.

(**Example:** every + where = everywhere)

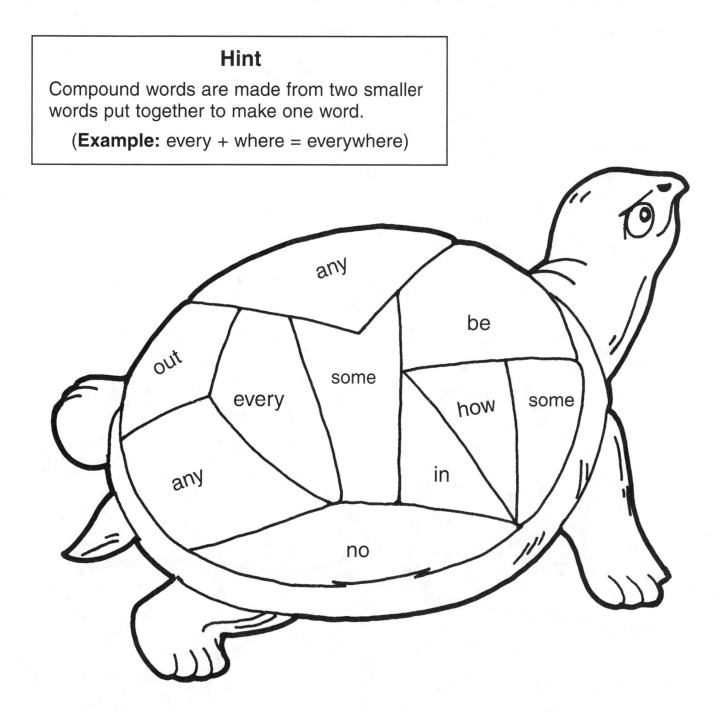

Cracked Compounds (cont.)

Turtle Shell Pieces

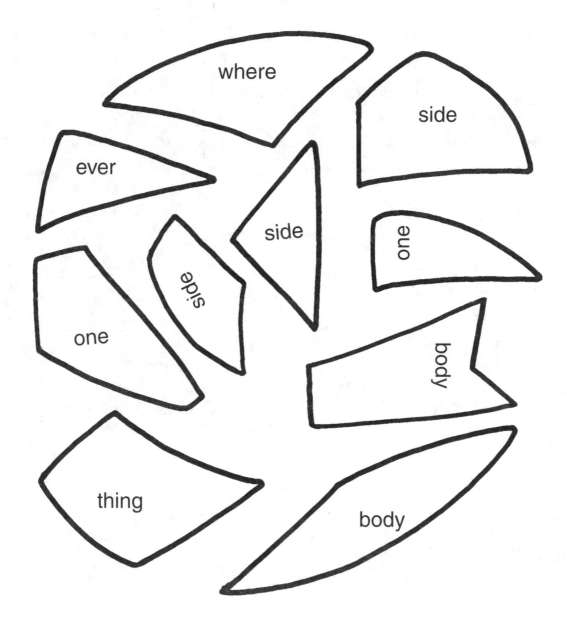

Contractions Resource List

Contractions are a shortened version of a word pair. The apostrophe is used to show where a letter or letters have been omitted to create the shortened form.

Contractions are a wonderful theme for a word wall. Here is a list to get you started. The following pages describe some activities for contractions, whether or not you should choose to do a related word wall.

Words with "not"

are not	aren't
cannot	can't
could not	couldn't
did not	didn't
do not	don't
had not	hadn't
has not	hasn't
have not	haven't
is not	isn't
should not	shouldn't
was not	wasn't
were not	weren't
will not	won't
would not	wouldn't

Words with "is"

he is	he's
it is	it's
she is	she's
that is	that's
there is	there's
who is	who's
what is	what's
where is	where's

Words with "would"

I would	I'd
he would	he'd
she would	she'd
you would	you'd
who would	who'd
they would	they'd

Words with "will"

I will	I'll
you will	you'll
he will	he'll
she will	she'll
we will	we'll
they will	they'll

Words with "has"

it has	it's
he has	he's
she has	she's
who has	who's
what has	what's
where has	where's

Words with "have"

I have	I've
you have	you've
we have	we've
they have	they've

Words with "are"

you are	you're
we are	we're
they are	they're

Words with "am"

I am	I'm

Words with "us"

let us	let's

CONTRACTIONS

Macaroni Contractions

Purpose

The students will practice using apostrophes, and they will recognize that contractions are made up of two words.

Materials

- Contractions Resource List (page 129)
- uncooked elbow macaroni
- construction paper or sentence strips
- markers or crayons
- scissors
- stapler

Preparation

Cut construction paper or sentence strips into 2" x 5" (5 cm x 13 cm) pieces.

Instructions

The student will choose a contraction he or she would like to build from the word list. On one side of a piece of paper, he or she will write the two words that make up the contraction. On the back side of the piece of paper, the student will write the contraction without the apostrophe. The student can trace over the letters with a marker or crayon. When the student is finished, he or she can practice placing a piece of macaroni in place of each missing apostrophe.

Students can make as many as time permits. Staple the pieces of paper together to form contraction booklets for the students.

Cleanup

Store the elbow macaroni in a resealable container. The students can keep their booklets in their desks or in a reading skills center for review.

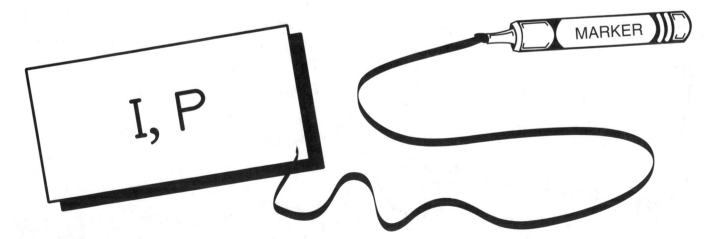

CONTRACTIONS

Contraction Word Trucks

Purpose

The students will match contractions to their original word pairs.

Materials

- copies of page 132
- Contractions Resource List (page 129)
- tagboard or construction paper
- markers
- scissors
- answer key (created by the teacher)

Preparation

Make copies of the truck and wheels on tagboard or construction paper. Cut out the pieces. Use a marker to write a contraction on the truck. On the wheels, write the words that form the contraction. Repeat this process for each of the trucks. Put all of the trucks and wheels in a manila envelope, and create an answer key.

Instructions

The student will lay out all of the contraction trucks and wheels. He or she will read the contraction on a truck (one truck at a time) and find the two wheels that contain the contraction's base words. For example, if the truck has the contraction *can't* on it, the student will find the wheels with *can* and *not* and place them on the truck. Have the students check their work with the answer key.

Cleanup

Store the trucks and their wheels in manila envelopes.

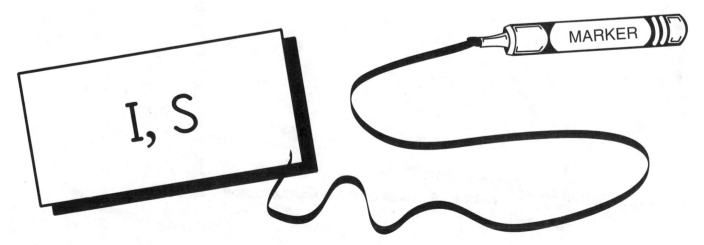

Contraction Word Trucks *(cont.)*

Truck and Wheel Patterns

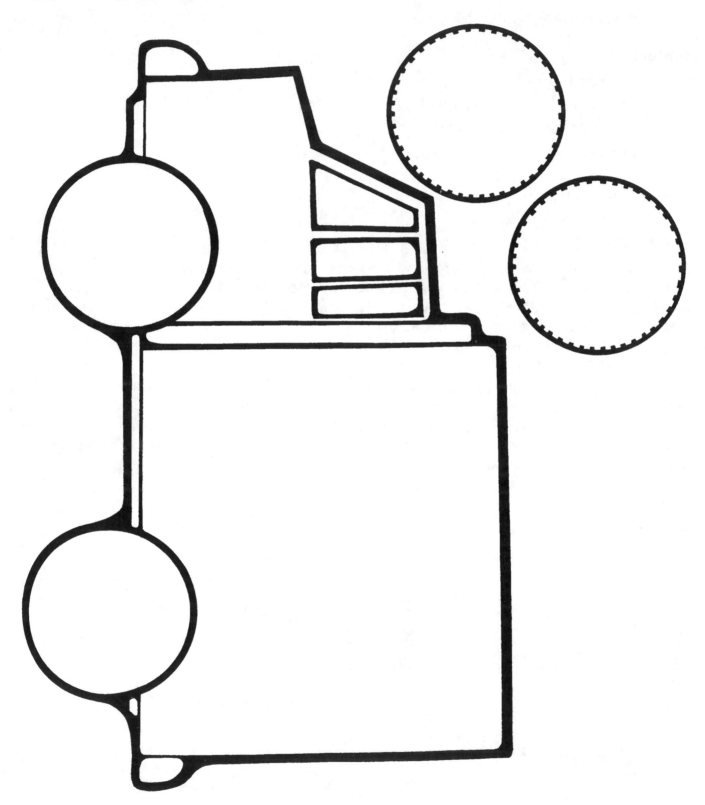

CONTRACTIONS
Computer Contractions

Purpose

Students will match contractions to their original word pairs.

Materials

- copies of pages 134 and 135
- Contractions Resource List (page 129)
- answer key (created by the teacher)
- markers
- laminating materials

Preparation

Make copies of pages 134 and 135. Use the cards on page 135. To create your own set of contractions, use the blank boxes on page 135 and write your words in before making the copies. Cut out the cards and laminate them if you wish. Prepare an answer key.

Instructions

The student will read one card at a time and place it on top of its matching contraction on the computer. When the student has placed all of the cards on the computer, he or she may check the matches with the answer key.

Cleanup

Collect the computer, its cards, and the answer key and place them in a manila envelope.

Variations

The students may wish to do this activity in the opposite direction. Instead of reading a card first and then searching the computer screen, they may read a word on the screen first and find its matching card.

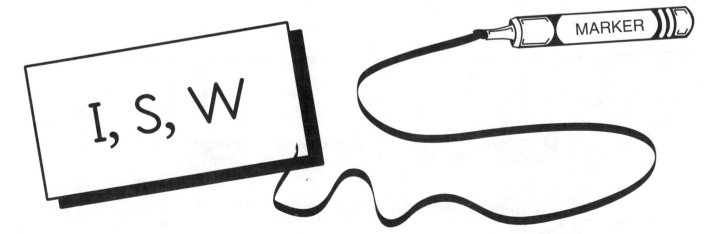

Computer Contractions *(cont.)*

Computer

you're   let's   you'll   didn't

he's   aren't   it's   she's

I'm   we're   I've   haven't

Computer Contractions *(cont.)*

Contraction Cards

you are	he is	I am	let us	are not
we are	you will	it is	i have	have not
she is	did not			

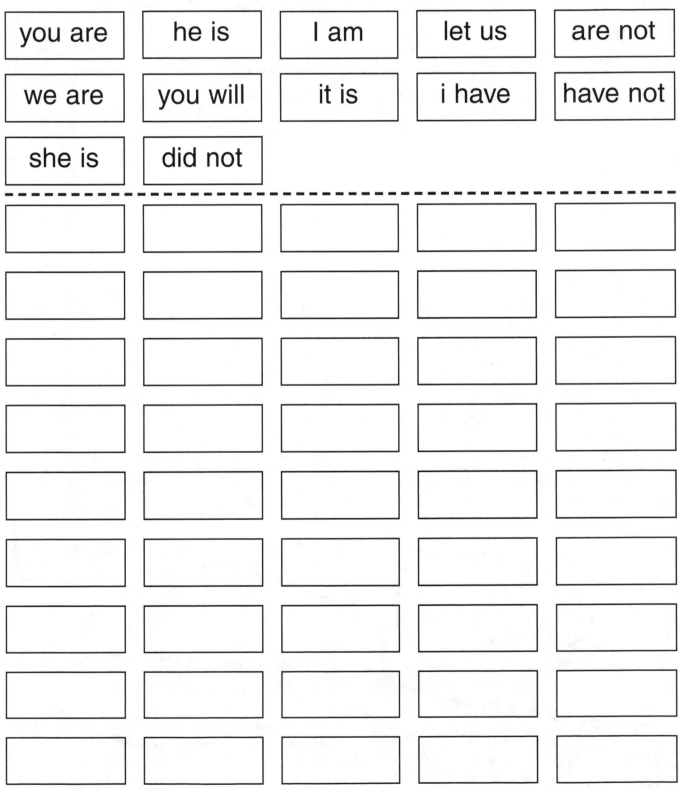

☐☐☐☐CONTRACTIONS☐☐☐☐

Contraction Magic

Purpose

Students will make flip books that change pairs of words into contractions.

Materials

- Contractions Resource List (page 129)
- construction paper of two contrasting colors, cut into 3" x 6" (8 cm x 15 cm) rectangles
- markers or crayons
- tape
- scissors
- stapler

Preparation

Cut construction paper into 3" x 6" (8 cm x 15 cm) pieces.

Instructions

Ask the students to choose a contraction that they would like to work on from the word list. Write the two words that make up the contraction on a piece of construction paper. Ask the students to write an apostrophe on another piece of paper and cut the strip long enough to cover the letters that will be dropped. Tape the apostrophe in place. By moving the apostrophe flap, the words will "magically" turn into their contraction form. The students can trace over the letters with markers or crayons. They can make as many contractions as time permits. Staple the pages together to form a booklet.

Cleanup

Make sure all of the markers are covered and the crayons are returned to their storage containers. Store the booklets in a place that the students can use them for reference.

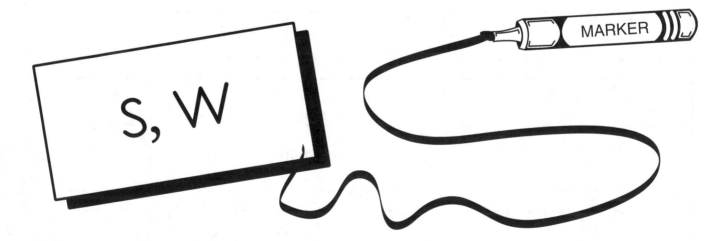

PREFIXES AND SUFFIXES

Prefixes and Suffixes Resource List

A **prefix** is a letter or a sequence of letters which is attached to the beginning of a word, root, or phrase to change its meaning.

A **suffix** is a letter or a sequence of letters which is attached to the end of a word, root, or phrase to change its meaning.

Prefixes and suffixes are a wonderful theme for a word wall. Here is a list to get you started. The following pages describe some activities for prefixes and suffixes, whether or not you choose to do a related word wall.

Prefix	Meaning
ante-	before
mid-	middle
anti-	against
mis-	wrong
bi-, bin-	two, twice
co-	together
out-	greater, better
de-	opposite of, remove from, reduce
over-	beyond, too much
post-	after
dis-	not, do the opposite of
pre-	before, in front of
en-	made of, belonging to, consisting of
re-	again
sub-	under, part of a whole
ex-	out
tele-	far away
fore-	in front of
trans-	move from one place to another
im-, in-, ir-	not
non-, un-	not
inter-	between
tri-	three
auto-	self
cent-	hundred
im-	into
micro-	small, short
semi-	half
super-	more than
under-	below

Prefixes and Suffixes Resource List (cont.)

Suffix	Meaning
-able, -ible	able to, capable
-al, -ant, -ent	belonging to, process
-ive, -ous	of action, relating to
-ance, -ence, -ancy, -ency	quality, act, or condition
-ant	to be or perform in a certain way
-ar	of or relating to, being
-ate	result of or act of
-er	person or thing belonging to or associated with, one that does or performs
-et, -est	superlative adjective
-ful	full of
-fy	to form into or become
-hood	state of being, membership in a group
-ie	like, pertaining to
-ist, -ant, -ent	person
-al, -ive, -ous	related to
-ics	study of, act or practice of
-ion	result of an act or process
-ish	nationality, having likeness to
-ive	having the quality
-less	without
-ly	in a certain manner
-ment	result of, action or process
-ness	manner or state of being
-or	one who does something, state or act
-ship	state of, office or skill
-tion, -sion	state of doing something
-ward	toward, in the direction of

PREFIXES AND SUFFIXES

Before and After

Purpose

Students will determine whether given words have prefixes or suffixes.

Materials

- construction paper or tagboard
- markers or colored pencils
- scissors
- glue
- copies of page 140–142

Preparation

Photocopy the combs on page 140. Cut out the comb cards, and mount them on construction paper or tagboard. Color the combs if you wish, and highlight the words on the cards by tracing them with a fine-tip marker. Copy the answer key (page 142) and page 141 and laminate them along with the comb cards.

Instructions

Students will read the word on each comb card and decide if it has a prefix or suffix. If the word has a prefix, the student will place it on the boy with the long hair. If the word has a suffix, the student will place it on the boy with the short hair. After all of the combs have been placed, the student may check his or her work against the answer key. To vary this activity, shuffle the word cards, and put them facedown. The students can draw one card at a time, read the word, and say whether the word has a prefix or suffix. Then they will place the cards in the correct categories. You may also wish to let students make their own comb cards by giving them blank outlines of the combs. Have them write on the combs five words that have prefixes and five words that have suffixes.

Cleanup

Store all of the materials in a large manila envelope.

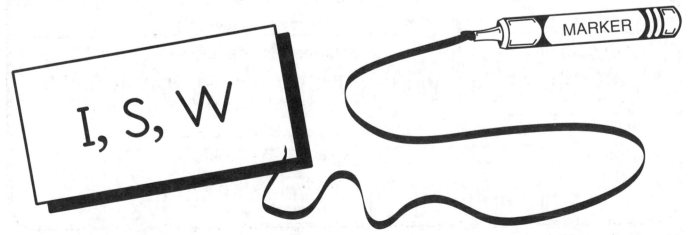

Before and After *(cont.)*

Comb Cards

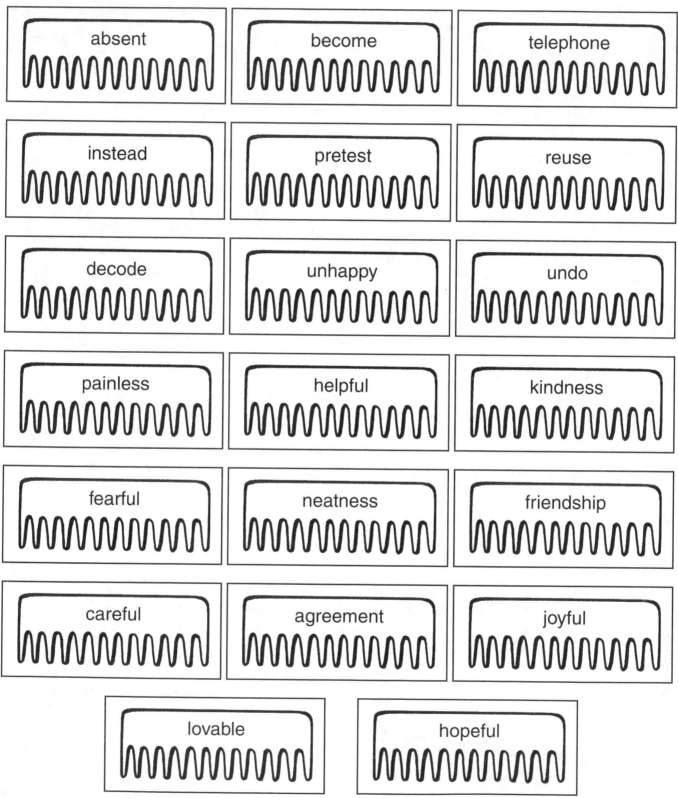

absent

become

telephone

instead

pretest

reuse

decode

unhappy

undo

painless

helpful

kindness

fearful

neatness

friendship

careful

agreement

joyful

lovable

hopeful

Before and After (cont.)

Before and After Game Board

Directions: If the word on the comb card has a prefix, place it on the boy with long hair. If the word has a suffix, place the comb card on the boy with short hair. Use the answer key on page 142 to check your work.

Suffix (After)

Prefix (Before)

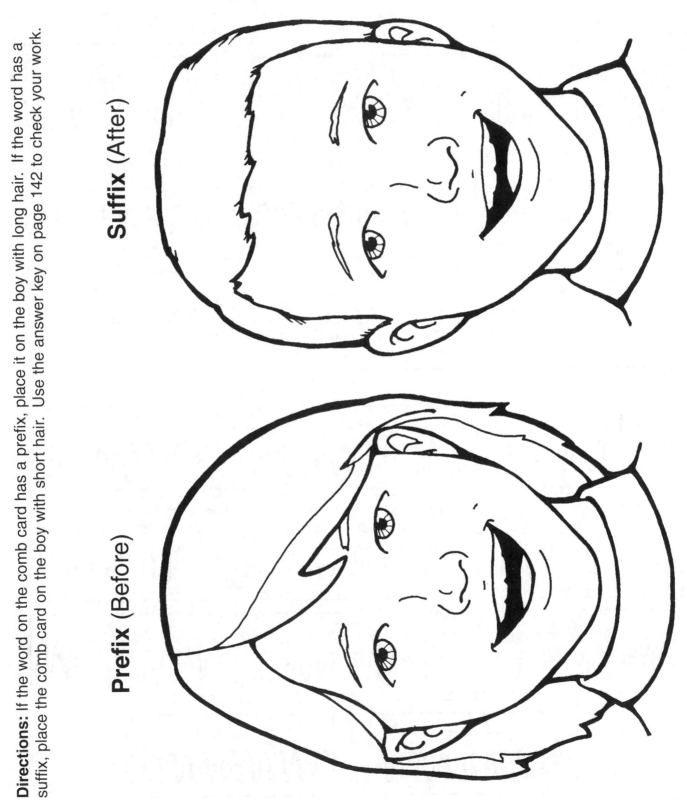

Before and After (cont.)

Before and After Answer Key

Prefixes

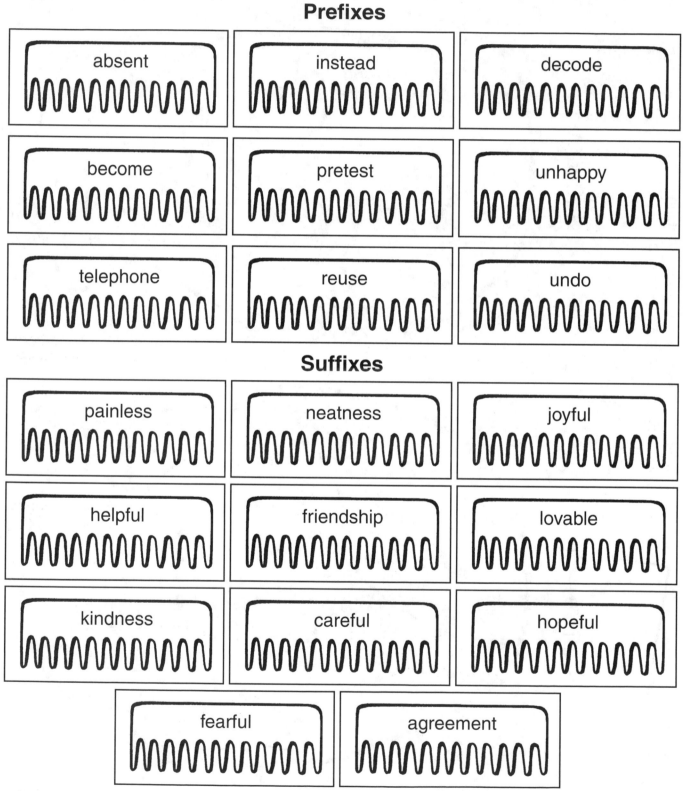

absent

instead

decode

become

pretest

unhappy

telephone

reuse

undo

Suffixes

painless

neatness

joyful

helpful

friendship

lovable

kindness

careful

hopeful

fearful

agreement

PREFIXES AND SUFFIXES

Prefixes and Suffixes on Your Word Wall

Purpose

Students will learn how prefixes and suffixes change the meanings of root words when they are added.

Materials

- Prefixes and Suffixes Resource List (pages 137 and 138)

- index cards

- marker

Preparation

Print each prefix and suffix that you are going to use on a separate index card. Make sure that the prefixes and suffixes are on two differently colored, sized, or shaped cards. Laminate them so they can be used again.

Instructions

Seat the students near the word wall. Call on individual students to place a prefix or suffix card next to a word on the word wall. If the prefix or suffix forms a new word, attach the card to that word. Discuss the meaning of the new word and ask a student to use it in a sentence.

Cleanup

Leave the prefix and suffix word cards on the word wall as long as you need. Otherwise, store them away to be used again.

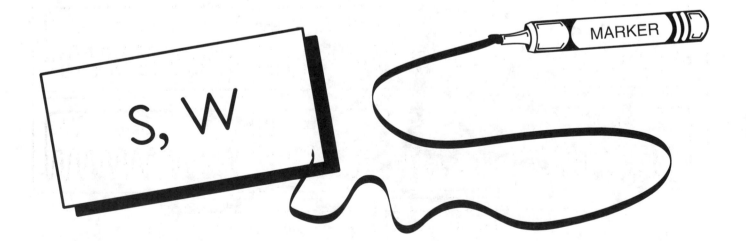

Missing Partners

Purpose

Students will make new words by adding prefixes and suffixes to root words.

Materials

- Prefixes and Suffixes Resource List (pages 137 and 138)

- 5" x 7" (13 cm x 18 cm) index cards

- marker

Preparation

Print predetermined root words, prefixes, and suffixes on index cards. Make enough so that everyone in your class will have at least one card.

Instructions

Give each student a card. Ask the students who have the root words to stand in a line. Then, ask the students with prefix or suffix cards to each find a root word partner. To be partners, the prefix or suffix must create a word when attached to the root word. When all of the students have paired up, have them read their words and use them in sentences.

Cleanup

Collect the cards and store them in a resealable plastic bag.

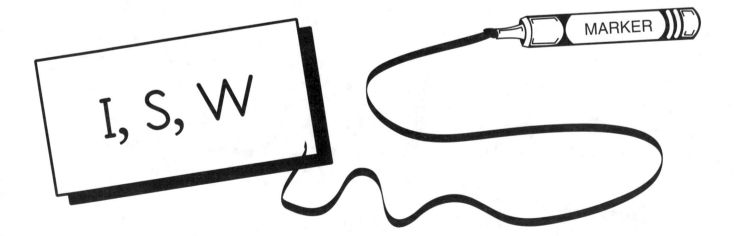

PREFIXES AND SUFFIXES

Prefixes and Suffixes in Print

Purpose

Students will identify prefixes and suffixes in different forms of reading material.

Materials

- Prefixes and Suffixes Resource List (pages 137 and 138)
- reading texts, social studies and science texts, newspapers, magazines, flyers, newsletters, etc.
- paper
- pencils
- stapler

Preparation

Post a list of prefixes and suffixes (pages 137 and 138) in your room where all the students can see it easily.

Instructions

Instruct students to search for prefixes and suffixes throughout their reading for one week. Tell them to keep a list of the words that they find and their sources.

At the end of the week, have the students staple their lists into books. Have them write "My Prefix and Suffix Book" on their covers.

Cleanup

The students can either keep their books or have them displayed in the class library.

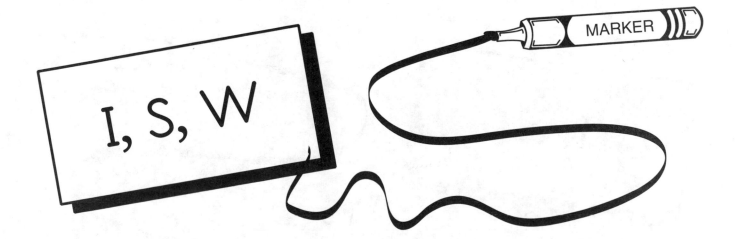

Prefix Train

Purpose

Students will make new words by adding prefixes to root words.

Materials

- construction paper or tagboard
- markers or colored pencils
- scissors
- glue
- laminating materials
- copies of pages 147 and 148

Preparation

Photocopy the train and wheel cards on pages 147 and 148. Cut out the wheel cards, and glue them onto circular pieces (the same size as the wheels) of construction paper or tagboard. Cut out the train cards and glue them onto construction paper or tagboard. Color the cards as you desire, using markers or colored pencils. Laminate them so they can be used again in the future. Copy the answer key and laminate it.

Instructions

Students will lay out all of the train cards on a table or the floor. Then they will match the root words (on the wheel cards) to the trains. A match is made when the prefix and root word create a new word. When they find a match, they will place the wheel on the train card. After all of the matches have been made, the students may use the answer key to check their work.

Cleanup

Store the train cards, wheel cards, and answer key in a manila envelope.

Variation

You may wish to ask the students to use the new words in sentences, either orally or in writing.

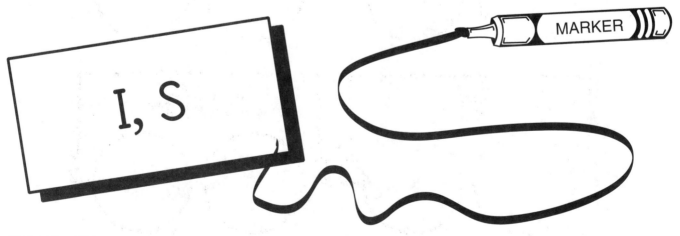

Prefix Train *(cont.)*

Train Cards

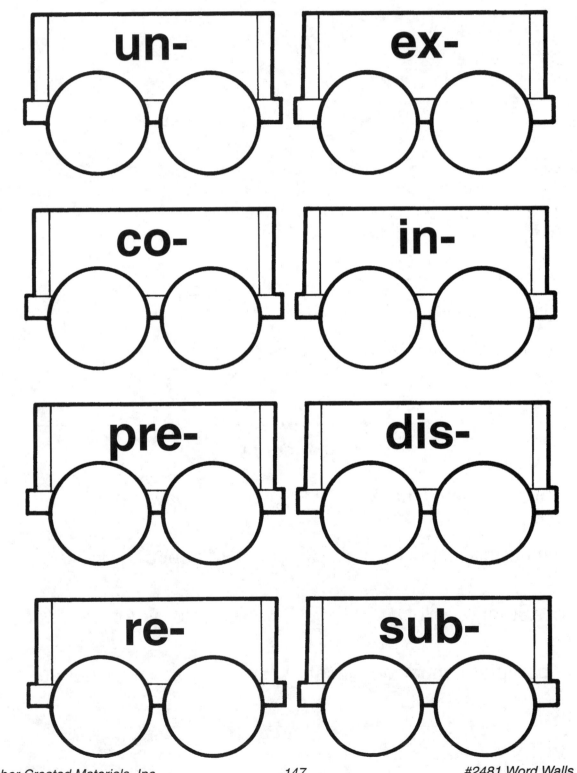

un-

ex-

co-

in-

pre-

dis-

re-

sub-

Prefix Train *(cont.)*

Wheel Cards

author

complete

fill

correct

turn

happy

way

marine

appear

like

set

pay

tie

pilot

change

plain

Answer Key

untie, unhappy, unlike

prepay, preset

exchange, explain

disappear, dislike

coauthor, copilot

refill, return, reappear, retie

incomplete, incorrect, inset

subway, submarine, subset

Flipping Over Suffixes

Purpose

Students will make new words by adding suffixes to root words.

Materials

- Prefixes and Suffixes Resource List (page 138)
- 2" x 6" (5 cm x 15 cm) pieces of construction paper or sentence strips
- 2" x 2" (5 cm x 5 cm) squares of tagboard or construction paper
- markers
- stapler
- scissors

Preparation

Cut a 2" x 6" (5 cm x 15 cm) piece of construction paper or sentence strip for each child. Then cut several 2" x 2" (5 cm x 15 cm) squares of tagboard for each child.

Instructions

The student will choose a root word to write on his or her 2" x 6" (5 cm x 15 cm) piece of construction paper. Then, the student will brainstorm suffixes that could go with the root word. He or she will print each suffix on a separate piece of the smaller paper. When the student has found as many suffixes as possible to go with the root word, he or she will stack them and staple them on the right end of the longer piece of construction paper or tagboard. Leave a blank square on top of the stack (to act as a cover) so that only the root word is visible. Students can trace their writing with markers. Allow students to share their words when everyone has finished.

Cleanup

The students could keep their booklets, or you could store them in a language arts corner for future review.

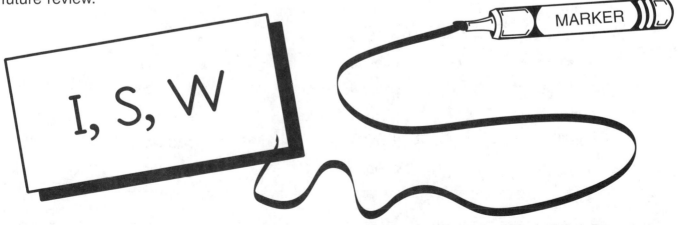

Homophones Resource List

Homophones are words that are pronounced the same way, but they are spelled differently and have different meanings. A homophone's meaning can be readily identified in the context of its sentence.

Homophones are a wonderful theme for a word wall. Here is a list to get you started. The following pages describe some activities for homophones, whether or not you should choose to do a related word wall.

ate/eight	groan/grown	plain/plane
be/bee	hair/hare	pray/prey
bare/bear	hall/haul	red/read
beat/beet	hear/here	road/rode
blew/blue	him/hymn	sail/sale
board/bored	hole/whole	sea/see
break/brake	hour/our	sew/so
buy/by/bye	knead/need	sight/site
carrot/carat	knew/new/gnu	soar/sore
cell/sell	knight/night	some/sum
cents/sense/scents	knot/not	son/sun
coarse/course	know/no	stair/stare
creak/creek	knows/nose	stake/steak
dear/deer	loan/lone	tacks/tax
do/due	made/maid	tail/tale
I/eye	mail/male	there/their/they're
fair/fare	meat/meet	threw/through
feat/feet	none/nun	to/too/two
flour/flower	oh/owe	wait/weight
for/four	one/won	waist/waste
forth/fourth	pail/pale	way/weigh
fir/fur	pair/pear/pare	weak/week
flea/flee	pain/pane	wood/would
grate/great	peace/piece	write/right

Homophone Match-Up

Purpose

Students will identify matching pairs of homophones.

Materials

- construction paper or tagboard
- scissors
- glue
- copies of pages 152–154
- laminating materials

Preparation

Make copies of pages 152–154. Cut out the sneaker cards on page 153. Mount the individual shoes on tagboard or construction paper rectangles of the same size. Laminate the sneaker cards and the game board.

Instructions

The students will spread the sneaker word cards out on a table or the floor. The first student will choose a sneaker card and read the word on it. He or she will then try to match the sneaker card to the appropriate homophones on the game board (page 152). Then play passes to the next student who tries to match a card to a sneaker on the page. The game is over when all of the homophone pairs have been matched together. Have the students check their answers against the answer key (page 154).

Cleanup

Put all of the activity materials in a manila envelope. Store the envelope in a language arts center.

Variations

For younger students, color each homophone pair the same color (both on the sneaker and the game board) for easy matching. Use as few or as many colors as you wish to aid your students.

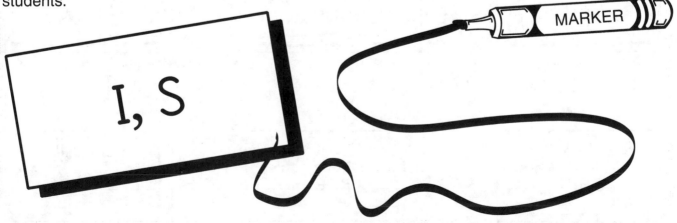

Homophone Match-Up *(cont.)*

Sneaker Game Board

 for

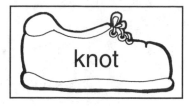 knot

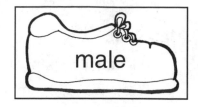 male

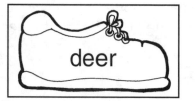 deer

 sea

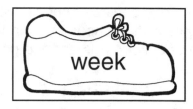 week

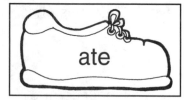 ate

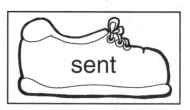 sent

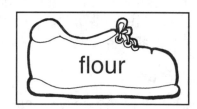 flour

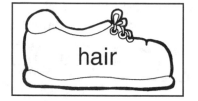 hair

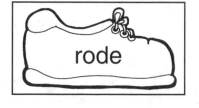 rode

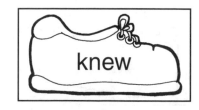 knew

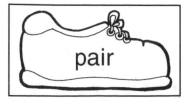 pair

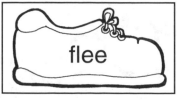 flee

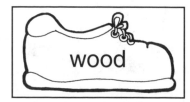 wood

Homophone Match-Up *(cont.)*

Sneaker Cards

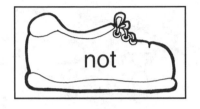

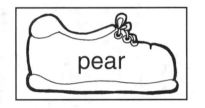

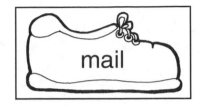

four

not

mail

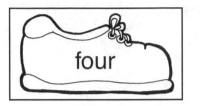

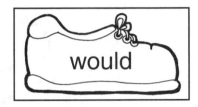

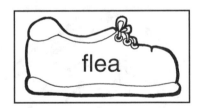

dear

pear

would

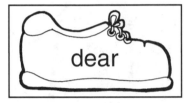

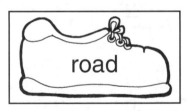

see

road

flea

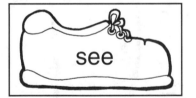

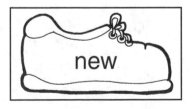

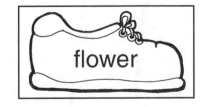

weak

new

flower

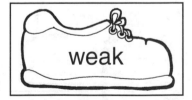

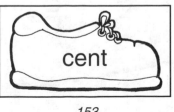

eight

cent

hare

Homophone Match-Up *(cont.)*

Sneaker Answer Key

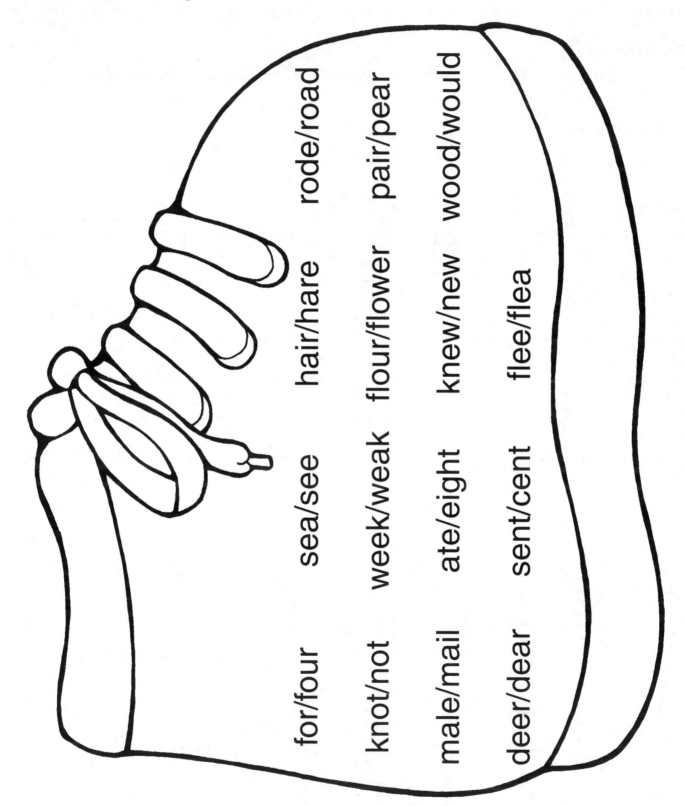

154

Homophone Search

Purpose

Students will identify homophones in everyday reading materials.

Materials

- reading books, social studies and science texts, magazines, newspapers, letters, flyers, etc.

- butcher paper or tagboard

- markers or crayons

Preparation

Post a blank piece of butcher paper or tagboard in your classroom where the students can have easy access to it. Place markers or crayons nearby.

Instructions

Ask the students to choose some form of reading material—a textbook, story, etc. Have the students search for words that are homophones. As they find them, have them write the words and their matches on the butcher paper or tagboard. Tell them to find as many as possible in a given amount of time. They can continue this activity in small groups or as an individual activity throughout the time you are focusing on homophones.

Cleanup

Store the reading materials in the appropriate places. You may also want to have a variety of reading sources near the poster so that the students can add to the list on their own.

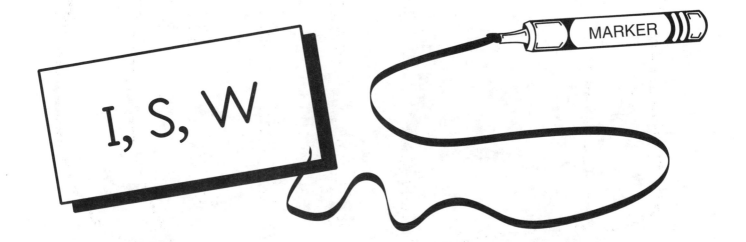

Draw a Homophone

Purpose

Students will show their understanding of the different meanings of the words in homophone pairs.

Materials

- Homophones Resource List (page 150)

- index cards

- crayons and markers

Preparation

Make a copy of page 150 or use a homophone list that you have brainstormed together in class.

Instructions

Give each student an index card. Tell the students to fold their index cards in half. Next they will each choose a pair of homophones that they would like to illustrate. Tell the students to write the homophone pair at the top of the index card, one word on each half. Next, they will illustrate the words. When they have done a predetermined number of cards, they can share their work in a group.

Cleanup

Post these cards in the room, in a pocket chart, or on a bulletin board.

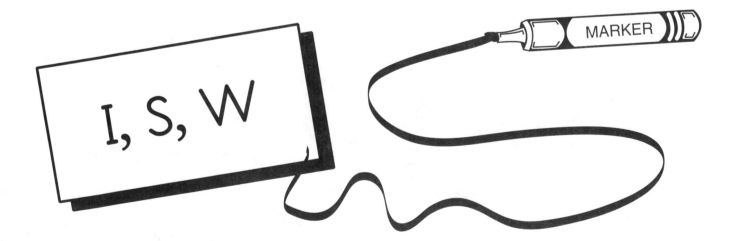

Hilarious Homophones

Purpose

Students will practice using homophones with their correct definitions.

Materials

- 2" x 18" (5 cm x 46 cm) sentence strips or construction paper

- markers or crayons

- scissors

- Homophones Resource List (page 150)

Preparation

Post the list of homophones (page 150) in the room. Cut paper or sentence strips into 2" x 18" (5 cm x 46 cm) rectangles.

Instructions

Hand out the strips to the students. Have them each choose a homophone pair and write it at the top of the strip. Each student will write on his or her strip one or two sentences which correctly use both words in the homophone pair. Have the students underline the homophones in their sentences. When everyone has finished, students can share their sentences with the class or in small groups.

Cleanup

Display the sentences around the classroom.

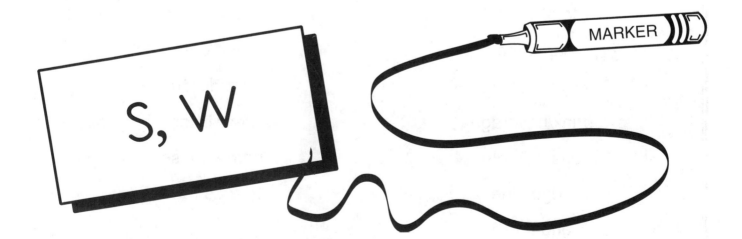

Synonyms Resource List

Synonyms are words with similar meanings.

Synonyms are a wonderful theme for a word wall. Here is a list to get you started. The following pages describe some activities for synonyms, whether or not you choose to do a related word wall.

above/over	false/untrue
afraid/scared	fast/quick
alike/same	fib/lie
angry/mad	find/discover
argue/fight	fix/repair
automobile/car	forest/woods
begin/start	forever/always
below/under	fresh/new
big/huge	friend/pal
boat/ship	funny/silly
city/town	gift/present
cool/cold	glad/happy
correct/right	go/leave
dad/father	good/great
dirty/filthy	hard/difficult
drink/beverage	hear/listen
easy/simple	home/house
edge/side	hurries/runs
end/finish	

Synonyms Resource List *(cont.)*

illustration/picture

incorrect/wrong

intelligent/smart

jump/hop

keep/save

late/tardy

laugh/giggle

like/enjoy

look/see

loud/noisy

man/gentleman

many/numerous

mom/mother

neat/tidy

nice/kind

odd/strange

pretty/lovely

rip/tear

road/street

sad/unhappy

say/tell

sea/ocean

shout/yell

skinny/thin

small/tiny

story/tale

student/pupil

surprised/startled

talk/speak

thing/object

throw/toss

tired/sleepy

waste/trash

wet/damp

yell/scream

Synonym Search

Purpose

Students will identify synonyms in everyday reading materials.

Materials

- reading books, social studies and science texts, magazines, newspapers, letters, flyers, etc.

- butcher paper or tagboard

- markers or crayons

Preparation

Post a blank piece of butcher paper or tagboard in your classroom where students can have easy access to it. Place markers or crayons nearby.

Instructions

Ask the students to choose some form of reading material—a textbook, story, etc. Have students search for words that are synonyms. As they find them, have them write the words and their synonym matches on the butcher paper or tagboard. Tell them to find as many as possible in a given amount of time. They can continue this activity in small groups or individually throughout the time you are focusing on synonyms.

Cleanup

Store the reading materials in the appropriate places. You may also want to have a variety of reading sources near the poster so that students can add to the list on their own.

SYNONYMS

Silly Synonym Nursery Rhymes

Purpose

Students will use synonyms to change the words in popular nursery rhymes.

Materials

- a collection of nursery rhymes
- large pieces of butcher paper
- markers
- paint and paintbrushes

Preparation

On a piece of butcher paper, write a sample nursery rhyme. Substitute synonyms throughout the nursery rhyme whenever possible. Paint an illustration at the bottom of the page. (See page 162 for an example.)

Instructions

With your students, recite a few favorite nursery rhymes. Ask the students to choose one and write it on the board. Then go through the poem line by line and replace words with their synonyms whenever possible. After the words have been substituted, read the completed nursery rhyme together. Discuss how the new version has the same basic meaning, even though it may not rhyme anymore. Then display the completed sample of your nursery rhyme.

Explain to the students that they will be writing and illustrating a nursery rhyme of their choosing (or you can pick it for them) in groups. Have them make their nursery rhymes and illustrations on butcher paper.

Cleanup

Wash the paintbrushes and put the paint away. Display the finished nursery rhymes around the room.

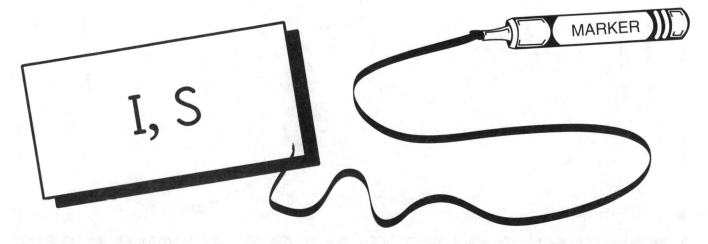

Silly Synonym Nursery Rhymes *(cont.)*

Variations

This activity is a great way to introduce a thesaurus and/or synonym dictionary to the students. Explain how to use them and have some available for their use.

Synonym Word Search

Purpose

Students will search for and read pairs of synonyms.

Materials

- copies of page 164 or 165 (if you choose to make your own puzzle)

- pencils

Preparation

Make copies of page 164 or create your own puzzle on page 165 and make copies of it.

Instructions

Have the students look for and circle synonym word pairs in the puzzle.

Cleanup

Ask the students to turn in the puzzles when they are finished. Correct the puzzles and return them to the students.

Variations

You can create your own word search on the blank puzzle on page 165. Include synonym word pairs that you use frequently in class.

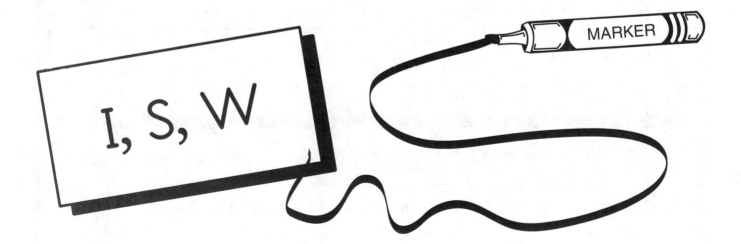

Synonym Word Search (cont.)

G	A	Q	Y	L	A	R	P	F	T	S	Q	U	I	Y	T	V	J	E	N	Z
B	S	J	A	S	T	A	R	D	Y	R	A	R	O	S	L	O	O	K	G	P
Z	A	M	K	B	H	E	M	N	E	T	Z	U	E	F	L	D	O	R	X	O
K	M	I	A	U	L	P	E	R	A	H	I	A	A	P	P	R	U	P	E	T
G	E	B	S	M	R	I	F	Z	P	T	F	O	Y	D	A	V	D	P	H	I
K	E	J	G	H	O	M	E	F	H	Y	R	A	B	E	Q	I	N	Q	A	N
I	O	O	W	T	N	U	L	Q	O	F	B	E	G	I	N	C	R	S	U	Y
X	T	O	K	J	L	N	A	E	C	L	U	D	M	P	Y	D	V	H	J	W
D	E	H	G	M	X	S	C	O	R	R	E	C	T	Y	G	L	M	O	C	Y
F	I	P	B	S	L	A	C	N	A	J	O	W	L	I	M	H	I	U	K	M
V	J	K	C	G	T	M	H	O	D	P	B	T	E	L	R	J	B	S	A	N
C	B	P	X	R	N	A	I	O	S	Z	I	G	P	A	Y	N	Y	E	N	I
S	M	A	L	L	U	H	R	A	L	R	I	G	H	T	P	J	H	C	E	F
I	T	H	J	S	W	Y	U	T	H	E	C	K	R	E	V	T	H	R	O	W
E	L	C	G	B	I	D	A	L	I	K	E	P	Q	T	F	O	D	T	N	O
H	F	T	M	E	G	R	E	U	B	L	G	E	P	L	V	R	E	M	K	M
S	E	R	O	V	L	U	K	S	A	B	W	U	S	C	E	U	A	V	O	X
E	K	N	J	C	X	S	O	S	T	F	Y	T	U	M	W	A	S	N	H	J
E	C	H	A	S	I	M	P	L	E	D	T	O	Z	C	T	W	Y	U	O	L
O	W	M	C	R	S	R	A	F	R	G	B	S	P	M	Q	N	P	N	R	O
S	D	K	R	S	V	D	U	L	B	T	V	S	D	Z	M	B	E	F	I	X

Look for the following synonyms in the above puzzle.

home/house	easy/simple	throw/toss
look/see	fix/repair	correct/right
alike/same	late/tardy	
begin/start	small/tiny	

Synonym Word Search (cont.)

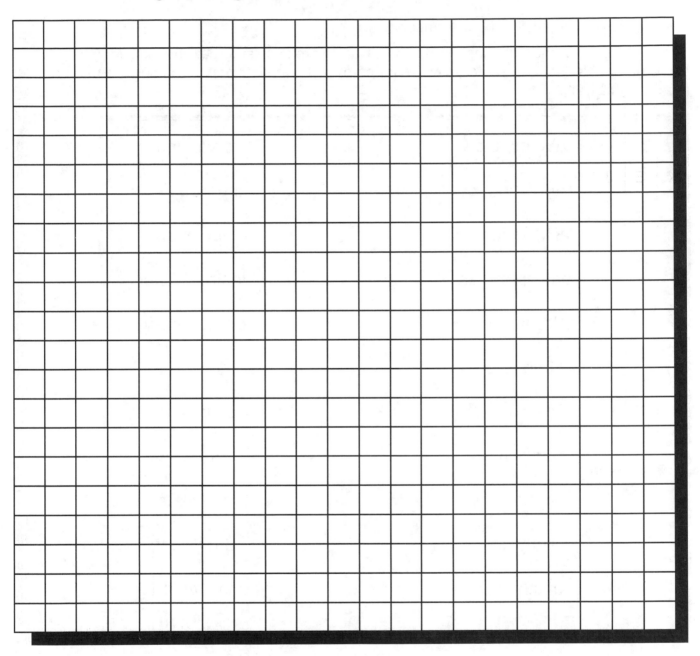

Look for the following synonyms in the above puzzle.

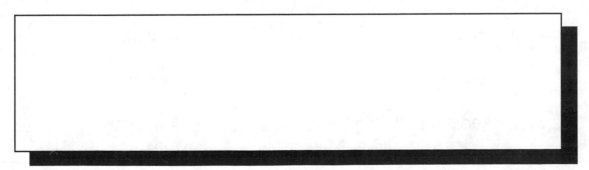

Antonyms Resource List

Antonyms are words with opposite meanings.

Antonyms are a wonderful theme for a word wall. Here is a list to get you started. The following pages describe some activities for antonyms, whether or not you choose to do a related word wall.

above/below	cry/laugh
add/subtract	dangerous/safe
alike/different	day/night
asleep/awake	destroy/repair
backward/forward	difficult/easy
bad/good	down/up
begin/finish	dull/sharp
big/little	dry/wet
black/white	early/late
buy/sell	east/west
catch/throw	enemy/friend
clean/dirty	exhale/inhale
close/open	false/true
cold/hot	fast/slow
come/go	fat/thin
crooked/straight	few/many

float/sink	noisy/quiet
forget/remember	north/south
found/lost	old/new
frown/smile	on/off
give/take	over/under
happy/sad	play/work
hard/soft	polite/rude
healthy/sick	pretty/ugly
hold/release	right/wrong
left/right	rough/smooth
light/dark	save/spend
loose/tight	short/tall
loud/quiet	sour/sweet
mean/nice	tame/wild
midnight/noon	terrible/wonderful
narrow/wide	whisper/shout

Antonym Search

Purpose

The students will identify antonyms in everyday reading materials.

Materials

- reading books, social studies and science texts, magazines, newspapers, letters, flyers, etc.

- butcher paper or tagboard

- markers or crayons

Preparation

Post a blank piece of butcher paper or tagboard in your classroom where the students have easy access to it. Place markers or crayons nearby.

Instructions

Ask the students to choose some form of reading material—a textbook, story, etc. Have the students search for words that are antonyms. As they find them, have them write the words and their antonym matches on the butcher paper or tagboard. Tell them to find as many as possible in a given amount of time. They can continue this activity in small groups or individually throughout the time you are focusing on antonyms.

Cleanup

Store the reading materials in the appropriate places. You may also want to have a variety of reading sources near the poster the students can add to the list on their own.

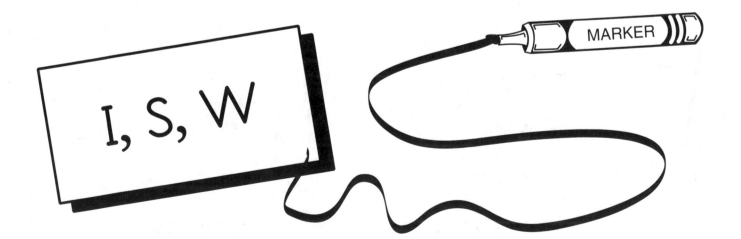

Antonym Concentration

Purpose

Students will identify pairs of antonyms.

Materials

- Antonyms Resource List (pages 166 and 167)

- index cards

- markers

Preparation

Choose some antonym pairs to use in this game. Write the antonyms on index cards (one word per card). Use a light marker so that the words do not show through to the backs of the cards. Laminate the cards for future use.

Instructions

This activity is a variation of the classic Concentration game. The students will place the word cards facedown in rows and columns. The first player will turn over two cards in an effort to find an antonym match. If the cards match, the player takes the cards and continues to play. If the cards do not match. The cards are turned back over and the next player takes a turn. The game continues until all of the pairs are found. The winner of the game is the one who has the most matched pairs.

Cleanup

Put the cards into an envelope and store them in a language arts or center.

Animated Antonyms

Purpose

Students will write sentences in which antonyms are correctly used.

Materials

- Antonyms Resource List (pages 166 and 167)

- paper

- pencils

- crayons or colored pencils

Preparation

Post the Antonyms Resource List somewhere in the room so that it is easily accessible to students.

Instructions

Give all students a piece of white paper. Ask students to each choose a pair of antonyms. The first word of the antonym pair will be written in a sentence on the front side of the paper. Its opposite will be written in a sentence on the backside of the paper. Ask students to circle or underline the antonyms. Students may then illustrate each sentence with colored pencils or crayons.

Cleanup

Compile the pages into a book titled "Animated Antonyms." Leave the book out for everyone to enjoy.

Variation

The students may use *Kid Pix Studio Deluxe* to create their own slides of antonyms. These may be complied into a class slide show.

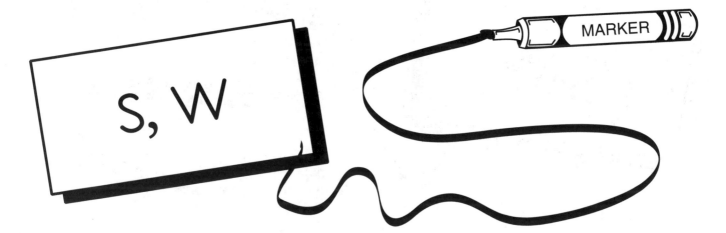

SYNONYMS AND ANTONYMS

Synonym and Antonym Review

Purpose

Students will review antonyms and synonyms.

Materials

- Synonyms Resource List (pages 158 and 159)

- Antonyms Resource List (pages 166 and 167)

- chalkboard or a dry-erase board

- chalk or dry-erase markers

Preparation

On the board, write a column of words from the synonym and antonym lists. In a second column, write the partners to the words in the first column. The second column should be in random order.

Instructions

Call a student up to the board and have him or her draw a line matching a synonym or antonym word pair. Ask the student to read the words aloud and say whether they are a synonym or antonym word pair. Continue until all of the pairs have been found.

Cleanup

Students may review the pairs aloud. Afterwards, erase the board.

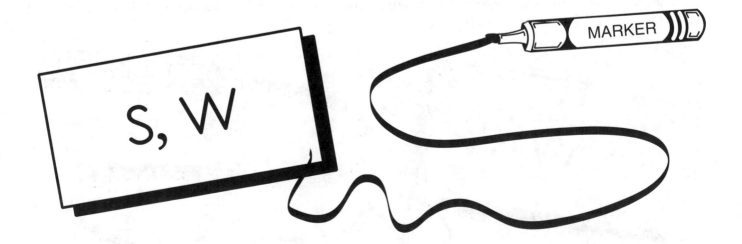

SYNONYMS AND ANTONYMS
Synonym and Antonym Chains

Purpose

Students will review synonyms and antonyms.

Materials

- 2" x 8" (5 cm x 20 cm) strips of construction paper in two colors

- crayons

- stapler

- Synonyms Resource List (pages 158 and 159)

- Antonyms Resource List (pages 166 and 167)

Preparation

Cut the construction paper into strips and have the synonyms and antonyms lists readily available for students.

Instructions

Students will write synonym and antonym word pairs on the strips. They will write one word on the front of each strip and one word (the first word's partner) on the back. Tell them to use two colors of paper: one for the antonyms and one for the synonyms. The students may use the antonym and synonym word lists or come up with their own pairs. When the strips have all been written on, interlock them into a chain and staple them together.

Cleanup

Use the chain to decorate your room.

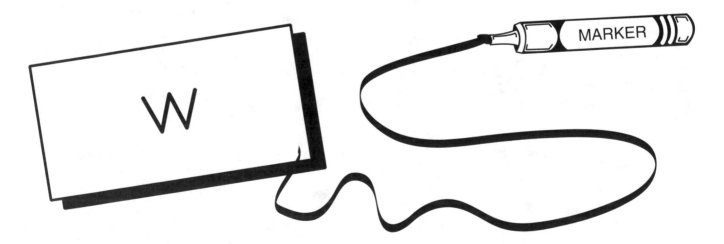

SYNONYMS AND ANTONYMS

Fishing for Synonyms and Antonyms

Purpose

Students will identify synonyms and antonyms.

Materials

- Synonyms Resource List (pages 158 and 159)

- Antonyms Resource List (pages 166 and 167)

- copies of page 174 and 175

- marker

- scissors

- glue

- file folder

- envelope

- answer key (made by the teacher)

Preparation

Copy as many fish as you will need (page 175). Write a word from a synonym or antonym pair on each individual fish. Cut out the two fishbowls (page 174) and glue them to the inside of a file folder. Label one fishbowl "Synonyms" and the other fishbowl "Antonyms." Cut out the fish and put them in an envelope. Put the envelope in the file folder. Label the outside of the folder "Fishing for Synonyms and Antonyms." Make an answer key for the word pairs and store it in the folder.

Instructions

The student will lay out all of the fish on the floor or a table. He or she will find two fish that either make up a synonym pair or an antonym pair. When a pair has been found, the student will put it on the appropriate fish bowl. The student can check his or her answers with the answer key after all of the pairs have been "caught."

Cleanup

Put all of the fish in an envelope. Store the envelope and the answer key in the file folder.

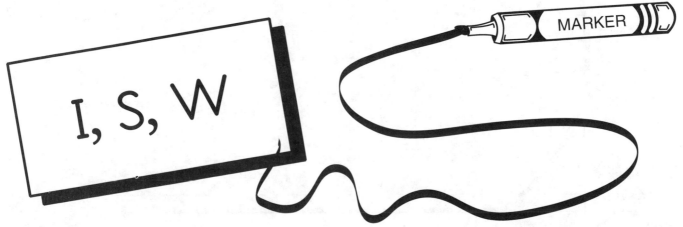

Fishing for Synonyms and
Antonyms *(cont.)*

Fishbowls

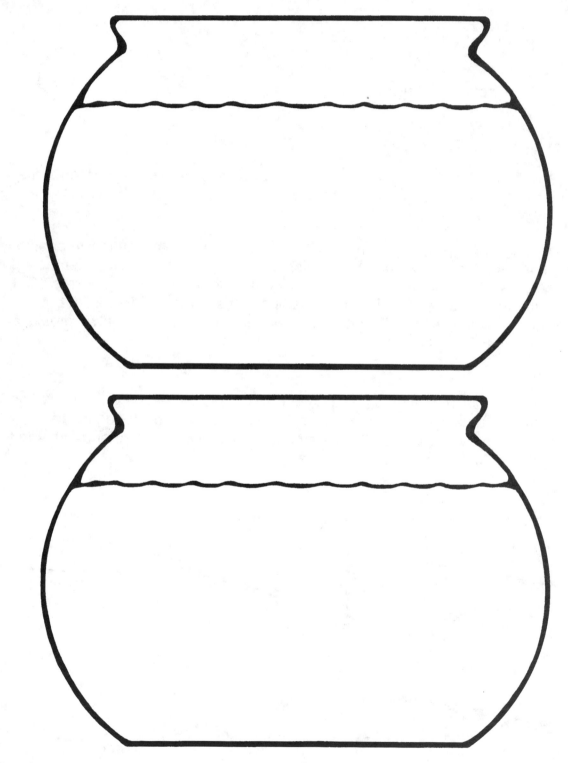

Fishing for Synonyms and Antonyms *(cont.)*

Fish

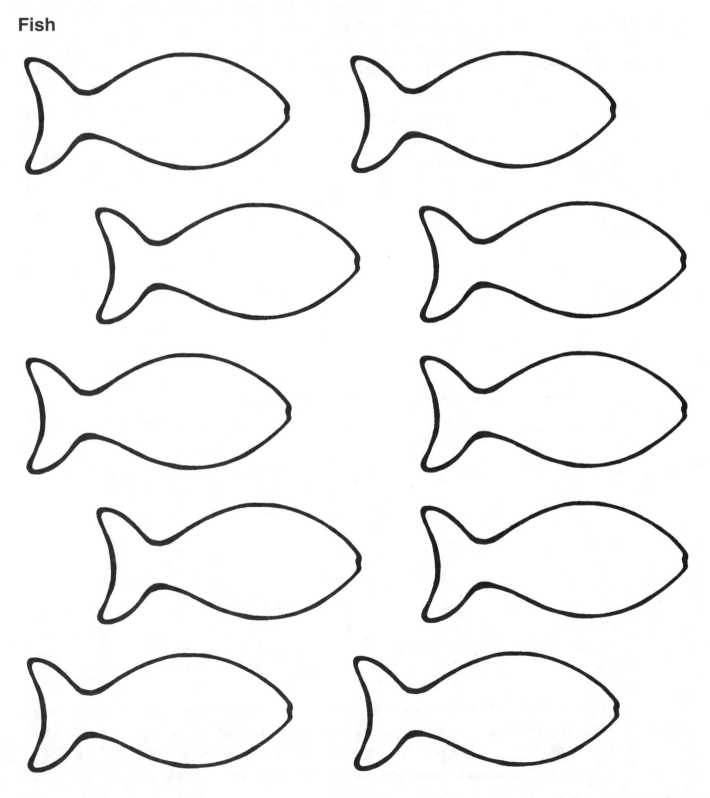

Word Families Resource List

Another type of word wall that you can have consists of words that have a particular pattern, specifically a rhyming phonetic pattern (word families). You can incorporate a word family into your regular word wall, or it can be a separate, smaller word wall, depending on your needs. The following are 37 rimes that are the basis of some word families.*

-ack	-at	-ight	-op
-ail	-ate	-ill	-ore
-ain	-aw	-in	-ot
-ake	-ay	-ine	-uck
-ale	-eat	-ing	-ug
-ame	-ell	-ink	-ump
-an	-est	-ip	-unk
-ank	-ice	-it	
-ap	-ick	-ock	
-ask	-ide	-oke	

*Pages 177–195 include these 37 rimes and selected literature that can be used to reinforce the word families. Several word family activities and games are provided on pages 196–202.

WORD FAMILIES

Word Families in Literature

-ack

back	pack	tack	snack
hack	rack	black	whack
jack	sack	crack	quack

- Causley, Charles. *"Quack," Said the Billy Goat.* (Candlewick, 1999)

- Cutts, David. *The House That Jack Built.* (Troll Books, 1979)

- Macaulay, David. *Black and White.* (Houghton Mifflin, 1990)

- Most, Bernard. *If the Dinosaurs Came Back.* (Harcourt Brace, 1984)

- Thaler, Mike. *The Teacher from the Black Lagoon.* (Scholastic, 1989)

-ail

hail	nail	sail	trail
jail	pail	tail	quail
mail	rail	frail	snail

- Carratello, Patty. *Gail's Paint Pail.* (Teacher Created Materials, 1996)

- Dubanevich, Arlene. *Tom's Tail.* (Viking, 1990)

- Heller, Ruth. *Kites Sail High.* (Grosset & Dunlap, 1988)

- McGovern, Ann. *If You Sailed on the Mayflower in 1620.* (Scholastic, 1993)

- Troughton, Joanna. *The Quail's Egg.* (Bedrick, 1988)

Word Families in Literature *(cont.)*

-ain

gain	rain	drain	stain
main	vain	grain	train
pain	brain	plain	strain

- Aardema, Verna. *Bringing the Rain to Kapiti Plain.* (Dial, 1992)

- Gibbons, Gail. *Trains.* (Holiday, 1988)

- Howard, Elizabeth Fitzgerald. *The Train to Lulu's.* (MacMillan, 1988)

- McPhail, David. *The Train.* (Little, Brown & Co., 1990)

- Pfister, Marcus. *Rainbow Fish.* (North-South Books, 1996)

-ake

bake	lake	take	shake
cake	make	wake	snake
fake	rake	flake	awake

- Baker, Keith. *Hide and Snake.* (Harcourt Brace, 1991)

- Carle, Eric. *Pancakes, Pancakes!* (Simon & Schuster Children's, 1998)

- Faulkner, Keith and Johnathen Lambert. *The Snake's Mistake.* (Price Stern Sloan, 1988)

- Hennessy, B. G. *Jake Baked the Cake.* (Puffin, 1992)

- Paschkis, Julie. *So Sleepy, Wide Awake.* (Owlet, 1997)

Word Families in Literature *(cont.)*

-ale

bale	kale	sale	stale
dale	male	tale	whale
gale	pale	scale	female

- Glimmerveen, Ulco. *A Tale of Antarctica.* (Scholastic, 1989)

- Potter, Beatrix. *The Tale of Benjamin Bunny.* (GT Publishing, 1997)

- Serventy, Vincent. *Whales and Dolphins.* (Scholastic, 1984)

- Slobodkina, Esphyr. *Caps for Sale.* (Scholastic, 1993)

- Wood, Audrey. *Little Penguin's Tale.* (Harcourt Brace, 1993)

-ame

came	game	same	flame
dame	lame	tame	frame
fame	name	blame	shame

- Bolognese, Don. *Little Hawk's New Name.* (Scholastic, 1995)

- Dantzer-Rosenthal, Myra. *Some Things Are Different, Some Things Are the Same.* (Random, 1990)

- Most, Bernard. *If the Dinosaurs Came Back.* (Harcourt Brace, 1978)

- Rylant, Cynthia. *The Relatives Came.* (Aladdin, 1993)

- Sadu, Itah. *Christopher Changes His Name.* (Firefly Books, 1998)

Word Families in Literature (cont.)

-an

ban	man	tan	plan
can	pan	van	scan
fan	ran	bran	than

- Anno, Mitsumasa. *Anno's Counting Book.* (HarperCollins, 1986)

- Berger, Barbara. *Grandfather Twilight.* (Paper Star, 1996)

- Carle, Eric. *Pancakes, Pancakes.* (Simon & Schuster, 1998)

- Farber, Norma. *There Was a Woman Who Married a Man.* (Addison-Wesley, 1978)

- Schmidt, Karen. *Gingerbread Man.* (Scholastic, 1985)

-ank

bank	tank	crank	spank
rank	blank	plank	thank
sank	clank	prank	shrank

- Allen, Pamela. *Who Sank the Boat?* (Paperstar, 1996)

- Gibbons, Gail. *Thanksgiving Day.* (Holiday House, 1985)

- McGovern, Ann. *The Pilgrims' First Thanksgiving.* (Scholastic, 1973)

- McKee, David. *Charlotte's Piggy Bank.* (Anderson Press Ltd., 1996)

- Warren, Mary P. *The Little Boat That Almost Sank.* (Concordia Publishing House, 1990)

Word Families in Literature *(cont.)*

-ap

cap	map	sap	clap
gap	nap	tap	snap
lap	rap	zap	trap

- Borden, Louise. *Caps, Hats, Socks, and Mittens.* (Scholastic, 1992)

- Cauley, Lorinda. *Clap Your Hands.* (Putnam, 1997)

- Rockwell, Anne. *Apples and Pumpkins.* (Aladdin, 1994)

- Slobodkina, Esphyr. *Caps for Sale.* (Scholastic, 1993)

- Wood, Audrey. *The Napping House.* (Harcourt Brace, 1984)

-ask

ask	task
bask	flask
mask	basket

- Burningham, John. *The Shopping Basket.* (Candlewick Press, 1997)

- Mora, Pat. *A Birthday Basket for Tia.* (Simon & Schuster, 1997)

- Mueller, Virginia. *A Halloween Mask for Monster.* (Viking Press, 1988)

- Rand, Gloria. *Baby in a Basket.* (Cobblehill, 1997)

- Rylant, Cynthia. *Eat It First, Ask Questions Later.* (Bradbury Press, 1985)

Word Families in Literature (cont.)

-at

at	fat	rat	flat
bat	mat	sat	scat
cat	pat	chat	slat

- Carle, Eric. *The Very Hungry Caterpillar.* (Scholastic, 1987)

- Cameron, Alice. *Cat Sat on the Mat.* (Houghton Mifflin, 1994)

- Nodset, Joan. *Who Took the Farmer's Hat?* (HarperCollins, 1963)

- Seuss, Dr. *The Cat in the Hat.* (Random, 1987)

- Seuss, Dr. *The Cat in the Hat Comes Back.* (Random, 1958)

-ate

ate	gate	rate	plate
date	late	crate	skate
fate	mate	grate	state

- Drescher, Henrik. *The Boy Who Ate Around.* (Hyperion, 1996)

- Kraus, Robert. *Leo the Late Bloomer.* (HarperCollins, 1994)

- Leet, Frank R. *When Santa Was Late.* (Ideals Publications Inc., 1990)

- Noble, Trinka Hakes. *The Day Jimmy's Boa Ate the Wash.* (Puffin, 1992)

- Salisbury, Kent. *A Bear Ate My Pear!* (McClanahan Book Co., 1998)

Word Families in Literature *(cont.)*

-aw

jaw	raw	draw	thaw
law	saw	flaw	crawl
paw	claw	straw	shawl

- Breinburg, Petronella. *Shawn Goes to School.* (HarperCollins, 1974)

- Carle, Eric. *Draw Me a Star.* (Putnam, 1998)

- Myers, Walter Dean. *How Mr. Monkey Saw the Whole World.* (Bantam, 1996)

- Seuss, Dr. *And to Think That I Saw It on Mulberry Street.* (Random House, 1997)

- Wildsmith, Bryan. *What the Moon Saw.* (Oxford University Press, 1987)

-ay

bay	hay	pay	way
day	lay	ray	clay
gay	may	say	play

- Baum, Arline and Joseph Baum. *One Bright Monday Morning.* (Random House, 1962)

- Brown, Margaret Wise. *The Runaway Bunny.* (HarperCollins Children's Books, 1991)

- Carlstrom, Nancy. *Happy Birthday, Jesse Bear.* (Simon & Schuster Children's, 1994)

- Cherry, Lynne. *Who Is Sick Today?* (Puffin/Unicorn, 1988)

- Gerson, Mary-Joan. *Why the Sky Is Far Away.* (Little, 1995)

Word Families in Literature *(cont.)*

-eat

eat	heat	seat	cleat
beat	meat	bleat	pleat
feat	neat	cheat	treat

- Barrett, Judith. *Cloudy with a Chance of Meatballs.* (Aladdin, 1982)

- Berenstain, Jan and Stan Berenstain. *Berenstain Bears Trick-or-Treat.* (Random House, 1989)

- Cohen, Miriam. *Don't Eat Too Much Turkey.* (Greenwillow, 1987)

- Sharmat, Mitchell. *Gregory the Terrible Eater.* (Simon & Schuster Children's, 1984)

- Sonneborn, Ruth. *Someone Is Eating Sun.* (Random House, 1974)

-ell

bell	fell	well	spell
cell	sell	shell	swell
dell	tell	smell	doorbell

- Egan, Louise. *The Farmer in the Dell.* (Whitman, 1987)

- Ets, Marie. *Elephant in a Well.* (Viking Press, 1972)

- Hutchins, Pat. *The Doorbell Rang.* (Morrow, 1989)

- Ryder, Joanne. *The Snail's Spell.* (Viking Press, 1988)

- Seagal, Lore. *Tell Me a Trudy.* (Farrar, Straus & Giroux, 1989)

Word Families in Literature *(cont.)*

-est

best	nest	west	quest
jest	test	chest	littlest
lest	vest	crest	slowest

- Chardiet, Bernice. *The Best Teacher in the World.* (Scholastic, 1991)
- Cohen, Miriam. *Best Friends.* (Simon & Schuster, 1989)
- Cohen, Miriam. *First Grade Takes a Test.* (Young Yearling, 1995)
- Jennings, Linda. *The Best Christmas Present of All.* (Dutton Books, 1996)
- Kroll, Steven. *The Biggest Pumpkin Ever.* (Scholastic, 1985)

-ice

ice	mice	price	twice
dice	nice	slice	thrice
lice	rice	spice	

- Baker, Alan. *Two Tiny Mice.* (Dial, 1991)
- Brandenburg, Franz. *Nice New Neighbors.* (Scholastic, 1990)
- Dooley, Norah. *Everybody Cooks Rice.* (Carolrhoda Books, 1991)
- Ivimey, John. *The Complete Story of the Three Blind Mice.* (Clarion, 1987)
- Sendak, Maurice. *Chicken Soup with Rice.* (Scholastic, 1992)

Word Families in Literature *(cont.)*

-ick

hick	nick	sick	brick
kick	pick	tick	chick
lick	quick	wick	trick

- Archambault, John and Bill Martin Jr. *Chicka, Chicka, ABC.* (Little Simon, 1993)

- Ginsberg, Mirra. *The Chick and the Duckling.* (Simon & Schuster, 1988)

- Ginsberg, Mirra. *Good Morning, Chick.* (Greenwillow, 1987)

- Kellogg, Steven. *Chicken Little.* (William Morrow & Company, Inc., 1985)

- Lionni, Leo. *Frederick.* (Knopf, 1967)

-ide

bide	side	bride	slide
hide	tide	glide	snide
ride	wide	pride	inside

- Balestrino, Philip. *The Skeleton Inside You.* (HarperCollins, 1989)

- Farber, Norma. *How to Ride a Tiger.* (Houghton Mifflin, 1983)

- Judd, Zachary. *Roller Coaster Ride.* (Silver Burdett & Ginn, 1992)

- McNulty, Faith. *How to Dig a Hole to the Other Side of the World.* (HarperCollins, 1990)

- Tresselt, Alvin. *Hide and Seek Fog.* (Lothrop, 1965)

Word Families in Literature *(cont.)*

-ight

fight	night	tight	fright
light	right	bright	knight
might	sight	flight	plight

- Allard, Harry. *Bumps in the Night.* (Bantam Skylark, 1984)

- Brown, Margaret Wise. *Good Night, Moon.* (Scholastic, 1993)

- Hazen, Barbara S. *Tight Times.* (Puffin, 1983)

- Moore, Clement C. *The Night Before Christmas.* (Random House, 1975)

- Tresselt, Alvin. *White Snow, Bright Snow.* (Scholastic, 1988)

-ill

ill	fill	pill	drill
bill	hill	will	grill
dill	mill	chill	skill

- Blair, Susan (retold by). *The Three Billy Goats Gruff.* (Holt, Rinehart and Winston, 1963)

- Carlstrom, Nancy White. *Jesse Bear, What Will You Wear?* (Scholastic, 1989)

- Ekker, Ernst. *What Is Beyond the Hill?* (Lippincott, 1986)

- Griffith, Helen. *Mine Will, Said John.* (Greenwillow, 1992)

- Langstaff, John. *Oh A-Hunting We Will Go.* (Simon & Schuster, 1991)

Word Families in Literature *(cont.)*

-in

bin	kin	tin	grin
din	pin	win	skin
fin	sin	chin	thin

- Allard, Harry. *Bumps in the Night.* (Bantam Skylark, 1984)

- Berenstain, Jan and Stan Berenstain. *Bears in the Night.* (Random House, 1971)

- Neitzel, Shirley. *The Jacket I Wear in the Snow.* (Greenwillow, 1989)

- Shaw, Nancy. *Sheep in a Jeep.* (Houghton Mifflin, 1989)

- Titherington, Jeanne. *Pumpkin, Pumpkin.* (Scholastic, 1999)

-ine

dine	mine	wine	twine
fine	pine	brine	whine
line	vine	spine	valentine

- Griffith, Helen. *Mine Will, Said John.* (Greenwillow, 1992)

- Hazen, Barbara Shook. *The Toad Is Mine!* (HarperCollins, 1998)

- Lionni, Leo. *It's Mine.* (Random, 1996)

- Ness, Evaline. *Sam, Bangs and Moonshine.* (Henry Holt, 1995)

- Schweninger, Ann. *Valentine Friends.* (Puffin, 1990)

Word Families in Literature *(cont.)*

-ing

ding	sing	cling	swing
king	wing	sling	spring
ring	bring	sting	thing

- Buchanan, Joan. *It's a Good Thing.* (Annick Press, 1984)

- Capucilli, Alyssa. *Good Morning, Pond.* (Hyperion, 1994)

- Mayer, Mercer. *There's Something in My Attic.* (Puffin, 1992)

- Reinl, Edda. *The Three Little Pigs.* (Neugebauer, 1983)

- Seidler, Ann and Jan Slepian. *The Hungry Thing Returns.* (Scholastic, 1990)

-ink

ink	mink	sink	drink
kink	pink	wink	think
link	rink	blink	shrink

- Joyce, William. *George Shrinks.* (HarperCollins Children's Books, 1998)

- Rayner, Mary. *Ten Pink Piglets.* (Dutton, 1994)

- Rossetti, Christina. *What Is Pink?* (Henry Holt, 1963)

- Seuss, Dr. *And to Think That I Saw It on Mulberry Street.* (Random, 1989)

- Seuss, Dr. *Oh! The Thinks You Can Think*! (Random House, 1975)

Word Families in Literature *(cont.)*

-ip

dip	sip	clip	skip
hip	tip	drip	ship
rip	chip	flip	trip

- Jonas, Ann. *Round Trip.* (Greenwillow, 1983)

- Parkinson, Kathy. *The Enormous Turnip.* (Whitman, 1987)

- Ransome, Arthur. *The Fool of the World and the Flying Ship.* (Farrar, 1968)

- Tryon, Leslie. *Albert's Field Trip.* (Atheneum, 1993)

- Winter, Jeanette. *The Christmas Tree Ship.* (Paperstar, 1998)

-it

it	hit	pit	slit
bit	kit	sit	skit
fit	lit	quit	split

- Borden, Louise. *Caps, Hats, Socks, and Mittens.* (Scholastic, 1992)

- Chapman, Cheryl. *Pass the Fritters, Critters.* (Four Winds Press, 1993)

- Grossman, Virginia. *Ten Little Rabbits.* (Chronicle, 1998)

- McDaniel, Becky. *Katie Did It.* (Children's Press, 1983)

- McPhail, David. *Fix It.* (Dutton, 1987)

Word Families in Literature *(cont.)*

-ock

dock	rock	clock	shock
lock	sock	flock	smock
mock	block	knock	stock

- Redhead, Janet. *The Big Block of Chocolate.* (Scholastic, 1989)

- Seuss, Dr. *Fox in Socks.* (Random House, 1966)

- Seuss, Dr. *There's a Wocket in My Pocket!* (Random House, 1974)

- Shone, Venice. *Cock-a-Doodle-Doo! A Day on the Farm.* (Scholastic, 1992)

- Van Laan, Nancy. *Possum Come A-Knocking.* (Knopf, 1990)

-oke

coke	woke	choke	stoke
joke	bloke	smoke	stroke
poke	broke	spoke	awoke

- Gifaldi, David. *The Boy Who Spoke Colors.* (Houghton Mifflin Co., 1993)

- Normand, Laura. *The Day the Computers Broke Down.* (Raintree Steck-Vaughn, 1997)

- Sargent, David. *Pokey Opposum.* (Ozark Publishing, 1996)

- Sneve, Virginia Driving Hawk. *When Thunders Spoke.* (University of Nebraska, 1993)

- Ziefert, Harriet. *When the TV Broke.* (Puffin, 1993)

Word Families in Literature *(cont.)*

-op

cop	pop	crop	prop
hop	top	drop	shop
mop	chop	flop	stop

- dePaola, Tomie. *The Popcorn Book.* (Holiday, 1984)

- Farber, Norma. *There Goes Feathertop.* (Unicorn-Dutton, 1979)

- Frost, Robert. *Stopping by Woods on a Snowy Evening.* (E. P. Dutton, 1978)

- Gomi, Taro. *Bus Stops.* (Chronicle, 1988)

- Seuss, Dr. *Hop on Pop.* (Random House, 1987)

-ore

ore	fore	sore	shore
bore	gore	tore	snore
core	more	wore	store

- Bassede, Francine. *George's Store at the Shore.* (Orchard Books, 1998)

- Gelman, Rita Golden. *More Spaghetti, I Say!* (Scholastic, 1993)

- Hutchins, Pat. *Clocks and More Clocks.* (Aladdin, 1994)

- Marshall, James. *George and Martha Encore.* (Houghton Mifflin, 1973)

- Morris, Jackie. *Bears, Bears, and More Bears.* (Barrons, 1995)

Word Families in Literature *(cont.)*

-ot

cot	hot	pot	blot
dot	lot	rot	knot
got	not	tot	spot

- Crews, Donald. *Ten Black Dots.* (Morrow, 1995)

- Demi, Hitz. *The Empty Pot.* (Holt, 1996)

- Hill, Eric. *Spot Goes to School.* (Putnam, 1984)

- Hill, Eric. *Where's Spot?* (Putnam, 1980)

- Mayer, Mercer. *I Just Forgot.* (Golden Books, 1988)

-uck

buck	muck	tuck	stuck
duck	puck	chuck	truck
luck	suck	cluck	struck

- Andersen, Hans Christian. *The Ugly Duckling.* (Golden Books, 1998)

- Charlip, Remy. *What Good Luck! What Bad Luck!* (Scholastic, 1969)

- Conover, Chris. *Six Little Ducks.* (Crowell, 1976)

- LeSieg, Theo. *I Wish I Had Duck Feet.* (Random House, 1965)

- McCloskey, Robert. *Make Way for Ducklings.* (Puffin, 1999)

Word Families in Literature *(cont.)*

-ug

bug	jug	tug	slug
dug	mug	drug	snug
hug	rug	plug	shrug

- Brown Ruth. *Ladybug, Ladybug.* (Puffin, 1992)

- Carle, Eric. *The Grouchy Ladybug.* (HarperCollins, 1996)

- Farber, Norma. *Never Say "Ugh" to a Bug.* (Houghton Mifflin, 1983)

- Fisher, Aileen. *When It Comes to Bugs.* (Harper, 1986)

- Greenberg, David. *Slugs.* (Little Brown, 1983)

-ump

bump	jump	clump	stump
dump	lump	grump	thump
hump	pump	plump	trump

- Arnold, Tedd. *No Jumping on the Bed!* (Dial, 1987)

- Baer, Gene. *Thump, Thump Rat-a-Tat-Tat.* (HarperCollins, 1991)

- Hayes, Sarah. *The Grumpalump.* (Clarion, 1991)

- Kalan, Robert. *Jump, Frog, Jump!* (Morrow, 1995)

- Walsh, Ellen S. *Hop Jump.* (Harcourt Brace, 1993)

Word Families in Literature *(cont.)*

-unk

bunk	junk	clunk	flunk
dunk	punk	chunk	skunk
hunk	sunk	drunk	shrunk

- Berenstain, Jan and Stan Berenstain. *The Berenstain Bears and Too Much Junk Food.* (Demco Media, 1985)

- Hoguet, Susan. *I Unpacked My Grandmother's Trunk.* (Dutton, 1983)

- Lavies, Bianca. *Tree Trunk Traffic.* (Puffin, 1993)

- McCloskey, Robert. *Make Way for Ducklings.* (Puffin, 1999)

- Turner, Ann. *Katie's Trunk.* (Simon & Schuster, 1992)

Magnetic Magic

Purpose

Students will use word families to make new words.

Materials

- magnetic alphabet letters (lowercase only)

- any magnetic board (Dry-erase boards are often magnetic.)

Preparation

Choose a word family to focus on. Line up the magnetic letters in alphabetical order across the bottom of the magnetic board. Write the base of the word family on the board or spell it out in magnetic letters.

Instructions

Call on students, one at a time, to come up and make all of the possible words that they can, using the magnetic letters. Start in order with the letter *a* and blend it together with the word base to see whether it makes sense or not. When a correct word has been discovered, write it on the board. Continue until all of the possible combinations have been found.

Cleanup

Store the magnetic letters in an envelope or plastic bag.

Variations

When a word is discovered, ask the students to write it down on paper. Then have them write sentences for the words.

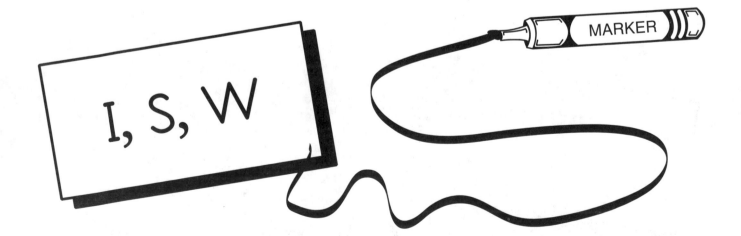

WORD FAMILIES
Silly Snake Race

Purpose

Students will blend letter sounds with word families to form new words.

Materials

- copies of pages 198 and 199
- game pieces
- dice
- crayons or markers
- construction paper or tagboard
- glue
- laminating materials
- dictionary

Preparation

Photocopy the game board on pages 198 and 199. Mount it on construction paper or tagboard. Color the game board if you wish and laminate it. Do not color in the center; leave it blank. After you have laminated the board, write the word family you want to concentrate on in the center (for example, *-at, -it, -ug*).

Instructions

Have the students put their game pieces at the starting position. The first player will roll the dice and move the number of spaces shown on the dice. When the player lands on a space, he or she will try to blend the letter on the space with the word family. If all of the players agree that a real word has been created, the player gets another turn. (**Note:** You might want to have a dictionary available in case the students need to verify whether or not a word is real.) If a word is not formed, the player stays in the space and the next player gets a turn. The game continues until someone reaches the snake's head.

Cleanup

Store all of the game pieces and the game board in a manila envelope.

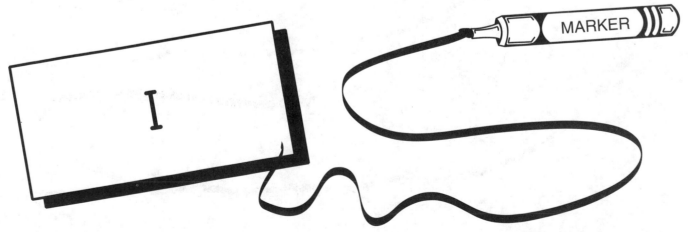

Game Board

Cut Here

Silly Snake Race (cont.)

Game Board (cont.)

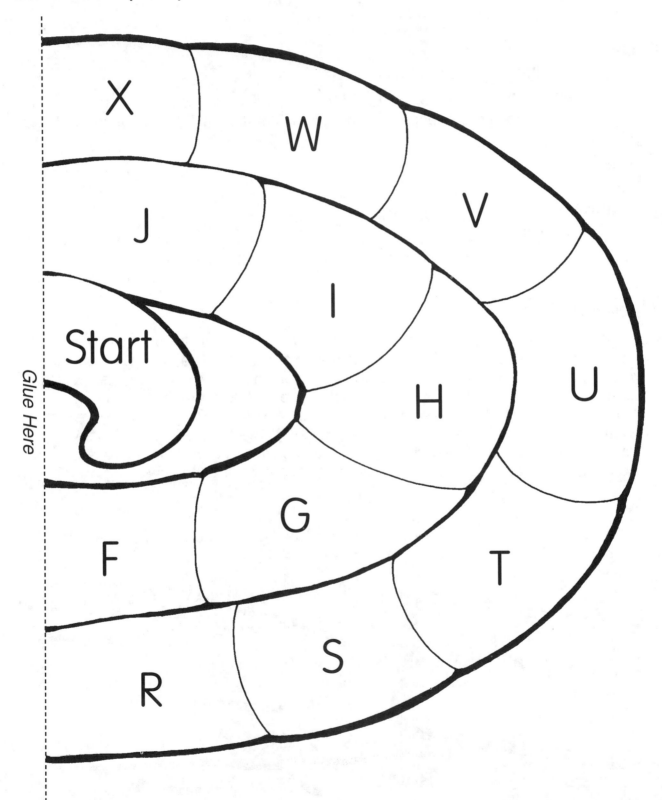

WORD FAMILIES
Word Family Bingo

Purpose

Students will practice identifying word families by playing a game.

Materials

- copies of page 201
- game markers (coins, poker chips, squares of paper, etc.)
- Word Families Resource List (page 176) and Word Families in Literature (pages 177–195)
- index cards
- marker

Preparation

Choose a word family that you want to focus on. Photocopy enough bingo cards for your whole class. Write the words from the chosen word family on individual index cards. Shuffle all of them together.

Instructions

Pass out the blank bingo cards to the students. Write the word family list on the board. Ask the students to randomly copy these words onto their bingo cards. They will need to write some words two to three times to fill in all of the squares. Then draw one index card at a time and read the word on it. (Or you may wish to hold up the card and let the students read it in unison.) The students will cover the word that has been called out with their game markers. The first player to get five in a row should shout, "Bingo!" Have the student read the words in the winning row back to you. If everything is correct, declare him or her the winner. If you would like the game to continue, ask the winner to come up and be the new caller.

Cleanup

If you would like to reuse the game boards and game markers, collect and store them in a manila envelope.

Word Family Bingo *(cont.)*

Bingo Card

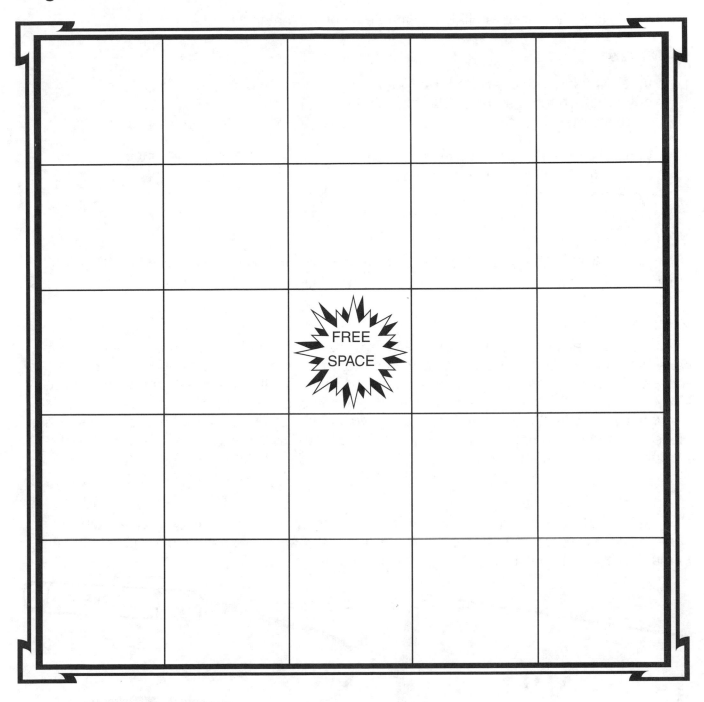

WORD FAMILIES

Cut and Paste Word Families

Purpose

Students will identify word families in everyday reading materials.

Materials

- magazines, newspapers, letters, flyers, any other written materials that the students may cut up

- Word Families Resource List (page 176) and Word Families in Literature (pages 177–195)

- scissors

- glue

- colored construction paper

Preparation

Choose a word family that you would like your class to focus on. Write the words from the family on the board. Cut the pieces of construction paper in half.

Instructions

Pass out the reading materials and construction paper to the students. Ask the students to write the base letters to the word family at the top of their construction paper (for example, *-at, -ug, -ice*). Have students search for words in the materials that belong to the word family. They may check the list on the board for help; however, encourage them to search for other words as well. When a student finds a word, he or she will cut it out and glue it on his or her piece of construction paper. Encourage students to find as many as possible in the given amount of time.

Cleanup

Repeat this activity with other word families during the course of the year. Store each student's lists in a separate folder. At the end of the year, staple each student's lists together to make a book. Label it "My Word Family Book."

Assessment Activities

Assessment activities will give you a quick overview of how your students are meeting your requirements. The following are some simple assessment activities that will show how well your students are mastering the words.

- Say several words from the word wall. Have the students point to the words.

- Point to several words on the word wall. Call on the students to read the words.

- Tell the students to number their papers one to five (or to any number you wish). Say five (or whatever number you chose) word wall words aloud, and have them write the words on their numbered papers.

- Help the students find sets of rhyming words on the word wall.

- Ask the students to find words that have like vowel sounds and/or consonant sounds on the word wall.

- Brainstorm with the students synonyms and/or antonyms for the word wall words.

- Ask the students to look for words on the word wall that have a certain number of syllables.

- Help the students find words that have prefixes and/or suffixes.

- Challenge the students to use several word wall words in a sentence, either orally or written.

- Tell the students to search for words with specific blends and/or digraphs.

- Say a definition to the students. Ask them to write down the matching word.

- Write a sentence on the board with a blank in it. Tell the students to use context clues to decide which word wall word is missing.

- The Ride the Word Waves activity on pages 16–23 can also be used to assess your students' progress with high-frequency words throughout the year.

600 Instant Words

These are the most often used words in reading and writing. The first 100 words are listed in order of frequency in Columns 1 through 4. Make sure that your students know most of these before teaching the second 100. Teach only a few at a time to keep the success rate high. Use these words for word walls, flash cards, games, spelling lessons, or just reading down the columns.

Column 1 Words 1–25	Column 2 Words 26–50	Column 3 Words 51–75	Column 4 Words 76–100	Column 5 Words 101–125	Column 6 Words 126–150
the	or	will	number	over	say
of	one	up	no	new	great
and	had	other	way	sound	where
a	by	about	could	take	help
to	words	out	people	only	through
in	but	many	my	little	much
is	not	then	than	work	before
you	what	them	first	know	line
that	all	these	water	place	right
it	were	so	been	years	too
he	we	some	called	live	means
was	when	her	who	me	old
for	your	would	oil	back	any
on	can	make	sit	give	same
are	said	like	now	most	tell
as	there	him	find	very	boy
with	use	into	long	after	following
his	an	time	down	things	came
they	each	has	day	our	want
I	which	look	did	just	show
at	she	two	get	name	also
be	do	more	come	good	around
this	how	write	made	sentence	form
have	their	go	may	man	three
from	if	see	part	think	small

600 Instant Words (cont.)

Column 7 Words 151–175	Column 8 Words 176–200	Column 9 Words 201–225	Column 10 Words 226–250	Column 11 Words 251–275	Column 12 Words 276–300
set	try	high	saw	important	miss
put	kind	every	left	until	idea
end	hand	near	don't	children	enough
does	picture	add	few	side	eat
another	again	food	while	feet	face
well	change	between	along	car	watch
large	off	own	might	miles	far
must	play	below	close	night	Indians
big	spell	country	something	walked	really
even	air	plants	seemed	white	almost
such	away	last	next	sea	let
because	animals	school	hard	began	above
turned	house	father	open	grow	girl
here	point	keep	example	took	sometimes
why	page	trees	beginning	river	mountains
asked	letters	never	life	four	cut
went	mother	started	always	carry	young
men	answer	city	those	state	talk
read	found	earth	both	once	soon
need	study	eyes	paper	book	list
land	still	light	together	hear	song
different	learn	thought	got	stop	being
home	should	head	group	without	leave
us	American	under	often	second	family
move	world	story	run	later	it's

 #2481 Word Walls Activities

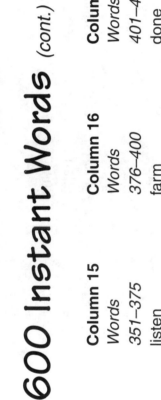

600 Instant Words *(cont.)*

Column 13	Column 14	Column 15	Column 16	Column 17	Column 18
Words	*Words*	*Words*	*Words*	*Words*	*Words*
301–325	*326–350*	*351–375*	*376–400*	*401–425*	*426–450*
body	order	listen	farm	done	decided
music	red	wind	pulled	English	contain
color	door	rock	draw	road	course
stand	sure	space	voice	half	surface
sun	become	covered	seen	ten	produce
questions	top	fast	cold	fly	building
fish	ship	several	cried	gave	ocean
area	across	hold	plan	box	class
mark	today	himself	notice	finally	note
dog	during	toward	south	wait	nothing
horse	short	five	sing	correct	rest
birds	better	step	war	oh	carefully
problem	best	morning	ground	quickly	scientists
complete	however	passed	fall	person	inside
room	low	vowel	king	became	wheels
knew	hours	true	town	shown	stay
since	black	hundred	I'll	minutes	green
ever	products	against	unit	strong	known
piece	happened	pattern	figure	verb	island
told	whole	numeral	certain	stars	week
usually	measure	table	field	front	less
didn't	remember	north	travel	feel	machine
friends	early	slowly	wood	fact	base
easy	waves	money	fire	inches	ago
heard	reached	map	upon	street	stood

600 Instant Words (cont.)

Column 19	Column 20	Column 21	Column 22	Column 23	Column 24
Words	*Words*	*Words*	*Words*	*Words*	*Words*
451–475	*476–500*	*501–525*	*526–550*	*551–575*	*576–600*
plane	filled	can't	picked	legs	beside
system	heat	matter	simple	sat	gone
behind	full	square	cells	main	sky
ran	hot	syllables	paint	winter	glass
round	check	perhaps	mind	wide	million
boat	object	bill	love	written	west
game	am	felt	cause	length	lay
force	rule	suddenly	rain	reason	weather
brought	among	test	exercise	kept	root
understand	noun	direction	eggs	interest	instruments
warm	power	center	train	arms	meet
common	cannot	farmers	blue	brother	third
bring	able	ready	wish	race	months
explain	six	anything	drop	present	paragraph
dry	size	divided	developed	beautiful	raised
though	dark	general	window	store	represent
language	ball	energy	difference	job	soft
shape	material	subject	distance	edge	whether
deep	special	Europe	heart	past	clothes
thousands	heavy	moon	sit	sign	flowers
yes	fine	region	sum	record	shall
clear	pair	return	summer	finished	teacher
equation	circle	believe	wall	discovered	held
yet	include	dance	forest	wild	describe
government	built	members	probably	happy	drive

If you would like more instant words for reading or spelling lessons, the entire list of 3,000 Instant Words can be found in the *Spelling Book, Words Most Needed Plus Phonics for Grades 1–6*. It is available from Phoenix Learning Resources, 468 Park Avenue South, New York, NY 10016 (800-221-1274).

References

Adams, M. J. *Beginning to Read: Thinking and Learning About Print.* (M.I.T. Press, 1990)

Bishop, A. and Bishop, S. *Phonics, Phonemic Awareness and Word Recognition* (Teacher Created Materials, 1996)

Clay, M. M. *Becoming Literate: The Construction of Inner Control.* (Heinemann, 1991)

Carrol, J. B., P. Davies, and B. Richman. *Word Frequency Book.* (Houghton Mifflin, 1971)

Cunningham, P. M. *Phonics They Use: Words for Reading and Writing.* (HarperCollins, 1995)

Eeds, M. *Bookwords: Using a Beginning Word List of High Frequency Words from Children's Literature K-3.* (*The Reading Teacher*, 38 (4) 418-423, 1985)

Gruber, B. and H. Chirinian. *Phonics and Reading.* (The Education Center, Inc., 1998)

Jacobs, W. J. and L. Nadel. *Stress-Induced Recovery of Fears and Phobias.* (*Psychological Review,* 92, 4:512–531, 1985)

Jensen, E. *Teaching with the Brain in Mind.* (Association for Supervision and Curriculum Development, 1998)

May, F. B. *Reading as Communication.* (Merrill Publishing Co., 1990)

McCracken, M. J. and R. A. McCracken. *Reading, Writing and Language: A Practical Guide for Primary Teachers.* (Peguis Publishers, 1995)

Stanovich, K. E. *Effects in Reading: Some Consequences of Individual Differences in the Acquisition of Literacy.* (Reading Research Quarterly, 21, 360–407, 1986)

Wylie, R. E. and D. D. Durrell. *Teaching Vowels Through Phonograms* (*Elementary English,* 47, 787–791, 1970)